For Ann, Dylan,

Cole and Noah...

who fill my life

with Gratitude!

CHOOSING GRATITUDE

Transforming Your Life & Community Despite the Odds

DENNIS R. ATWOOD

Choosing Gratitude

Transforming Your Life & Community Despite the Odds

books@marketsquarebooks.com

141 N. Martinwood, Suite 2 Knoxville, Tennessee 37923

ISBN: 979-8-9942008-0-3

Printed and Bound in the United States of America

Editor: Sheri Carder Hood

Cover Design: Kevin Slimp

Page Design: Ashley Burton

Contents

Preface

I'm going to let you in on a little trade secret in case you haven't already noticed. If left to their own devices, many preachers often preach on topics they themselves struggle with. And that is why I have turned to the Revised Common Lectionary for almost all of my ministerial career. The Lectionary provides an Old Testament reading, a psalm, a Gospel passage, and an Epistle reading for the preacher to select from as the Spirit leads. In addition, it helps keep the preacher honest by looking at the whole of Scripture over a three-year cycle. It also provides a sense of unity with millions of Christians across the globe each week as we dive into the same grouping of scripture passages and journey through the Christian year.

However, from time to time, I have wandered off the Lectionary path and addressed topics related to life together as a congregation, usually preaching a sermon series in the summer or fall.

This book arose out of a sermon series on "Gratitude." Yes, my congregation probably needed to hear it, but little did I know that I was really preaching to myself. You see, I was diagnosed with early onset Parkinson's disease at the age of fifty-four and was doing great the first six or seven years. I had no idea about the struggles that lay ahead. As the disease decided to progress, it was as if I had suddenly fallen off a cliff.

So, the truth is, most days, I struggle and fail to choose gratitude. In short, having Parkinson's sucks because it takes so much away from you. I try to have more days that I choose gratitude than days when Parkinson's wins. This tends to happen most when I am doing something that benefits others who may also be traveling a difficult road.

So, in this book, I try to honestly confess my personal journey into gratitude while living with Parkinson's and try to show that it is not just an inward journey. Rather, the gratitude journey ultimately expresses itself in sharing that joy and thanksgiving with others, particularly by engaging with the poor in the community. Christian gratitude is both an inward and an outward transformation.

I must also note how Parkinson's affects the entire family—which causes me to feel a bit guilty and sad sometimes that this ugly, uninvited intruder has disrupted my family life and vocation. Thankfully, I have an amazing wife who promised to love me "in sickness and in health," until we are parted by death, and three young adult sons who are talented, intelligent, and compassionate. And for them, I am beyond grateful.

I also want to express my gratitude to Bryan King, Doug Courchene, and Sonya O'Brien, who spent many hours together as The Gratitude Project Committee—sometimes making difficult decisions. And without Bryan as our chairperson, how lost we would have been.

Finally, I am grateful for the people—many who are great saints gone before us— who, over twenty-two years, allowed me the privilege of serving as their pastor.

And now, I invite you to join me on this journey of choosing gratitude every day of your life while making a positive impact in your community where it is needed the most.

Dennis Atwood

Introduction

The intent of this book is simply to provide inspiration and aspiration. In these pages, I will argue that personal gratitude must lead to meaningful action in our communities. The book is intended for individual study, small-group studies, congregation-wide studies, book clubs, social and community service groups, or you can simply grab a couple of friends to read and discuss the reflection questions together over coffee. Although I write from a congregational perspective, please do not limit this transformational model to the traditional church. God is at work in the world everywhere, and the big takeaway is that genuine personal gratitude necessarily leads to engagement with the most vulnerable among us—"the least of these," as Jesus called them. Gratitude cannot be privatized, nationalized, or institutionalized.

Again, this book is not just for congregations—because the reality today is that church membership in the United States has been in a significant decline for the past twenty years. I know firsthand, having spent thirty years of my life trying to revive two congregations—one in the Midwest and the other in the Southeast—with little numerical success. In the process, I presided over a couple of hundred funerals and welcomed fewer new church members and baptisms each year.

The fact is, fewer Americans are identifying as members of religious congregations than ever before. This decline is often attributed to population shifts—especially from rural to urban areas—and to younger generations being less likely to join churches than their predecessors. But a very real and significant portion of the decline is due to individuals with religious affiliations leaving formal membership, also known as the "dechurched," those who are burned out on the institutionalism of the church and the hypocrisy of its leaders and membership.

According to Gallup, "U.S. church membership was 70% or higher from 1937 through 1976, falling modestly to an average of 68% in the 1970s through the 1990s. The past 20 years have seen an acceleration in the drop-off, with a 20-percentage-point decline since 1999 and more than half of that change occurring since the start of the current decade."[1]

We need fresh approaches. Questions must be honestly contemplated, such as:

- What do you, your church, or group do well?
- What are your strengths?
- What assets does your congregation, or group, already possess in terms of finances, properties, and the giftedness of the people?
- What are the biggest needs in your community?
- Who is being underserved and overlooked?
- Where are the gaps that exist between services being

[1] https://news.gallup.com/poll/248837/church-membership-down-sharply-past-two-decades.aspx, accessed November 12, 2025.

provided and the people who need basic, affordable housing, food, family support, educational resources, and job opportunities?

These are just some of the questions for you to consider on your own journey. I believe that all ministry is contextual. So, you must do the work of discovering what incarnational ministry looks like in your own context of community. As you discover innovative ways to reframe your mission and purpose in your community, there is a good chance that you and those around you will find your lives transformed by God's Spirit.

The Gratitude Project, which I will discuss in the second half of the book, is an example of a small congregation in rural eastern North Carolina impacting its community in a big way by sharing its assets with a spirit of gratitude—expecting nothing in return. Their ambitious goal is to contribute to the broader effort to alleviate poverty, build strong families, strengthen education, and foster a spirit of hope and community. I will share a framework for getting started that you can adapt and tailor to the context of your own community. You are in the best position to discern God's Spirit in a way that impacts the neediest parts of your community through an asset-based approach.

"Gratitude" is defined as "the quality of being thankful; a readiness to show appreciation for and to return kindness."[2] Kindness—in this day and time? Sounds like a radical concept, right?

---

2 Oxford Languages, s.v. "gratitude," accessed November 12, 2025, https://languages.oup.com/google-dictionary-en/.

Actually, it is, and it must begin within us. There is no other way around it. Gratitude must begin within you and me first, and it can only come from God's Spirit transforming us. Maybe now more than ever, the American church needs genuine gratitude expressed in kindness and mercy as we relearn how to love our neighbors as ourselves—the second most important commandment of all.

It seems that in our current culture, our default mode is anger, division, and judgment. And all too often, the church mirrors the culture. But, brothers and sisters, this ought not be so! When did "loving your neighbor" and "showing hospitality to strangers" become "woke" concepts that needed to be canceled? In our present day, pastors offend many in their own congregations by simply preaching from Jesus' own Sermon on the Mount. No wonder churches of every denomination and across every theological spectrum are declining or on life support.

Much has already been written and researched regarding the decline of the American church over the past several decades. So, I will leave that story for others to analyze and dissect. What I am hopeful about today are the opportunities we have before us to reinvent ourselves as local congregations and as people outside the traditional church. Our task is to become more authentically the people that Jesus intended us to be.

As Kenda Creasy Dean rightly observes in her book *Innovating for Love:*

> *One of the things hampering 21st century congregations—which have become obsessed with their many shortcomings—has been our insistence on asking, "How can we build a better church?" That is the wrong question. The real question is, "Are we the people Christ calls us to be?"—*

human beings in communion with God and one another. Our model—and indeed our power-source—for such a compassion-driven, grace-drenched version of humanity is Jesus.

We are not called to build better churches. We are called to be better at being human, better reflections of God's love, formed in communities of people stumbling toward Jesus, squinting in the dazzling sunlight of new life.[3]

Becoming better at being human reflections of God's love involves becoming people of genuine gratitude, compassion, and action. This means we must intentionally cultivate congregations filled with imperfect people who exude genuine gratitude—people who serve and worship the God of abundance, not scarcity.

In Part One, I share a bit of my personal story and six meditations that lay the groundwork for biblical gratitude, offered for your inspiration and reflection. These illustrations are intended to help cultivate a heart of gratitude, which must be experienced inwardly before it can be authentically expressed in our attitudes, words, and actions.

Letting go of our small imaginations and scarcity-based outlooks is essential for cultivating genuine gratitude. These meditations can be used for personal devotions, small-group study, or Sunday morning classes with questions for reflection and action at the end of each chapter.

In Part Two, I share the story of First Baptist Church

---

3 Kenda Creasy Dean, *Innovating for Love: Joining God's Expedition through Christian Social Innovation* (Knoxville, TN: Market Square Publishing, 2021).

of Mount Olive, North Carolina, where I served as senior pastor for twenty-two years. Steps of our journey toward "The Gratitude Project" are laid out for application and aspirational purposes. This is just one practical example of innovation coming from a small group of people in a small town, and I hope it will open the eyes of ordinary people to the possibilities of transformation in their own particular communities. Creative use of church properties and space for the benefit of local communities is also a part of this transformative process.

Ultimately, I hope you will be inspired to stir up some "good trouble" in your congregation and community by thinking outside the traditional box and developing a "posture of possibilities" for what can be as we participate in the work of the kingdom of God.

There is a simple joy and freedom that is possible from God's Spirit when we practice gratitude in our personal lives, resulting in freely sharing our resources with our neighbors.

> *Now to him, who by the power at work within us is able to accomplish abundantly far more than all we can ask or imagine, to him be glory in the church and in Christ Jesus to all generations, forever and ever. Amen.*
>
> **Ephesians 3:20-21 (NRSV)**

Part One:

Cultivating Gratitude Within Us

John Lewis

"Get in good trouble, necessary trouble, and help redeem the soul of America."

John Lewis

CHAPTER ONE
Choosing Gratitude

O come, let us sing to the Lord; let us make a joyful noise to the rock of our salvation! Let us come into his presence with thanksgiving; let us make a joyful noise to him with songs of praise! For the Lord is a great God, and a great King above all gods. In his hand are the depths of the earth; the heights of the mountains are his also. The sea is his, for he made it, and the dry land, which his hands have formed.

O come, let us worship and bow down, let us kneel before the Lord, our Maker! For he is our God, and we are the people of his pasture and the sheep of his hand. O that today you would listen to his voice!

Do not harden your hearts, as at Meribah, as on the day at Massah in the wilderness, when your ancestors tested me, and put me to the proof, though they had seen my work. For forty years I loathed that generation and said, "They are a people whose hearts go astray, and they do not regard my ways." Therefore in my anger I swore, "They shall not enter my rest."

Psalm 95 (NRSVue)

On September 29, 2024, I preached my final sermon to a congregation I loved and served for twenty-two years. The reason for my departure was not how I had envisioned it ending. No, I was not being fired. I was stepping down because I could no longer fulfill my calling—physically.

Eight years earlier, I had been diagnosed with early-onset Parkinson's disease at age fifty-four. Parkinson's is a degenerative neurological condition for which there is no cure.

For the first six or seven years, the medications I was taking did their job of fighting off the symptoms of Parkinson's.

The only people who knew about my diagnosis were my wife and a couple of family members. Rightly or wrongly, I considered sharing my diagnosis publicly to be a career killer. We didn't even tell our three young adult sons until just a few months before I shared the news with my congregation.

I had been athletic all my life, running dozens of road races, including a marathon and several triathlons. I played golf regularly and enjoyed hunting and the great outdoors. I coached my sons through many baseball and basketball seasons as they grew up. I had always been very physically active, but now I was at a new crossroads. I had to admit my limitations. And a big part of coming to terms with this sense of powerlessness was the unexpected grief of leaving the pastoral life of over thirty years.

The time came for my final sermon, and I wrestled with what to say. The congregation had heard me preach for twenty-two years, so there was nothing left for me to say except thank you. I thanked them for putting up with me and for being patient with me, especially as I battled back problems and Parkinson's disease. I thanked them for their generosity, compassion, and support as I moved into The Great Unknown, and I thanked them for loving my family. For all those years, they had allowed me into their lives in the most joyous and the most gut-wrenching, painful times, and for that, I was so grateful.

I expressed my gratitude to them for allowing me to try new things and innovate because sometimes we need to stir up a little "good trouble," as the late John Lewis said during the Civil Rights Movement. The Gratitude Project was probably my biggest ASK, but the congregation stepped up and made a positive impact on our community in a variety of ways, strategically investing $100,000 in the poorest parts of Mount Olive.

First Baptist demonstrated that a small church can do BIG things for the kingdom of God. We weathered floods, hurricanes, and a recession. We managed occasional disagreements, renovated our buildings, and added a Christian Life Center. We entered into the solar farming business, began welcoming Haitian immigrants into our community in 2012, and provided space for Creole worship services. We navigated changes in staff, survived a pandemic, all while learning to be a post-COVID church in a very politicized, polarized culture.

And THAT, friends, describes *life* together in the church: flawed human beings doing our best—most of the time—stumbling after Jesus wherever he leads us. So, with all the good, a little bad—and the occasional ugly—among the challenges and opportunities, and after twenty-two years as their friend and pastor, I told them that I was choosing gratitude as my lens for looking backward and for moving forward into that liminal space between the "now and the not yet." I hope you will choose gratitude in your life as well.

In her book titled *Grateful: The Subversive Practice of Giving Thanks,* Diana Butler Bass writes, "Gratitude researchers claim that if we are grateful, we are happier and more content," and that there is a "social consequence to thankfulness." But she contends, "Other data say we are angry, discontented, and unsatisfied. And our politics isn't exactly based in gratitude."

Butler Bass explains, "Thank you doesn't seem to be our strength right now." There is a gap between what we believe and what we practice. This is the gratitude gap. We may be thankful in private, but individual gratefulness does not appear to make much difference in our larger common life. She continues: "Giving thanks may be personally rewarding, but larger forces have extinguished beneficial forms of gratitude from our economic and political lives ... We recognize gifts and are grateful on a [personal basis] but the world in which we live is surely not shaped by such thankfulness ... we live in a toxic habitat of ingratitude ... and nothing really escapes its poison."[4]

So, I wonder how we might begin to close the gap between our personal gratitude and our collective life together? Maybe it boils down to intentionally choosing gratitude over the toxic forces of cynicism, fear, hate, anger, division, discontent, bitterness, resentment, and complaint—because things will never be perfectly set up to our liking, and there are no perfect people in this imperfect world we live in. But how can we cultivate more gratitude? For starters, the psalmist says, "Come, let us sing for joy to the Lord ... Let us come before him with thanksgiving and extol him with music and song" (Psalm 95:1-2, NIV).

The fact is, giving thanks has always been one of the most central acts of worship for the people of God. Psalm 95 is a song of thanksgiving, along with a warning attached that was a part of the temple liturgy. It's a call for the people to worship the God who is both creator of the world and creator of the people of Israel.

---

[4] Diana Butler Bass, *Grateful: The Subversive Practice of Giving Thanks* (Harper One, 2018).

The first part of the hymn (vv. 1-5) was sung as the congregation moved toward the temple in a procession. Imagine them all singing "Let us come into his presence," as they processed. The second part (vv. 6-7) was sung as the people entered into the sacred halls of the temple in response to the first part—"O come, let us worship and bow down."

The opening words of the psalm tell us to "come" and "sing"—two verbs. The summons to praise in Psalm 95 is based upon the mighty works God has already done in the past.

But apparently, Israel's present religious life was characterized by too much comfort and confidence in its status as God's chosen people. They were remembering the past but failing to connect with the present!

After the people processed into the temple for worship, at the conclusion of the opening hymn, a priest pronounced the second part of the psalm with a very abrupt transition into a solemn solo, or chant, issuing a prophetic warning. It must have been a very jarring experience moving from a lively, joyous anthem to the grave solo chant of a priest. And the transition was meant to drive home a point. It was a warning.

After the seven verses of praise and thanksgiving comes the prophetic warning to the people, "O that today you would listen to his voice!" The rest of the psalm provides us with a negative example of the people of Israel rebelling against God at Meribah and Massah.

This incident was just one of many in which the Israelites contended with God during the Exodus period and wilderness wanderings in Exodus 17. This is why God came to refer to Israel as a "stiff-necked people," and the wilderness came to represent the worst of Israel's character traits—*stubbornness, ingratitude, and complaining.* And because the people did not regard the ways of God, they wandered for forty years in the wilderness.

The Israelites were always forgetting that their worship of the one true God and King—who had delivered them in the past—must then move them to an obedience of God's will in the present.

Just as the people continually grumbled and complained in the wilderness with Moses, despite God's provision for them, we also tend to forget God's blessings and provision for us. When that happens, we become blind to our blessings and lose the sense of wonder and joy that gives birth to genuine gratitude. God has certainly blessed us and called us to be a blessing to our entire community.

Psalm 95 is meant to cultivate gratitude among the people of God in every time and place, culminating in acts of love, service, and compassion with "the least of these," the most vulnerable people in society.

In choosing gratitude, we are also compelled to speak up for those who have no voice, to be agents of God's love and reconciliation, to stand in solidarity with the poor and oppressed, and to be the "salt of the earth and the light of the world," as Jesus says.

In my farewell sermon at First Baptist, I offered two challenges:

- Choose gratitude as your lens for looking at your life, the church, and the world.
- Let that gratitude propel you to continue to be the "presence of Christ" in fresh new ways in this community and beyond for many years to come.

And with that, my pastoral career was over—at least as

far as my eyes can presently see. I am still choosing gratitude as my lens through which to see the world, although I know nothing about where this road might lead.

"A Prayer of Unknowing" by Thomas Merton has meant a great deal to me through the years, but it has an especially deeper meaning attached for me today:

My Lord God,

I have no idea where I am going. I do not see the road ahead of me.

I cannot know for certain where it will end.

Nor do I really know myself,

and the fact that I think I am following Your will

does not mean that I am actually doing so.

But I believe that the desire to please You does in fact please You.

And I hope I have that desire in all that I am doing.

I hope that I will never do anything apart from that desire.

And I know that, if I do this,

you will lead me by the right road,

though I may know nothing about it.

Therefore, I will trust You always

though I may seem to be lost and in the shadow of death.

I will not fear, for You are ever with me,

and You will never leave me to face my perils alone.

Amen.[5]

---

[5] Thomas Merton, *Thoughts in Solitude* (New York: Farrar, Straus and Giroux, 1958).

Reflection and Action

1. Reflect on a time in your life that did not turn out the way you had envisioned. How did you handle that disappointment? Did you find it possible to choose gratitude as your lens for viewing your situation? Why or why not?

2. What are several healthy ways to help others through difficult times?

3. What are some destructive patterns that might hinder a spirit of gratitude and compassion?

4. Name a few examples of "bad theology" that you have heard said from well-meaning Christians to those going through difficult times.

5. Read "A Prayer of Unknowing" by Thomas Merton out loud. What words or phrases connect with you at this present time?

CHAPTER TWO

Gratitude in Anxious Times

In our age everything has to be a "problem." Ours is a time of anxiety because we have willed it to be so. Our anxiety is not imposed on us by forces from outside. We impose it on our world and upon one another from within ourselves.[6]

Thomas Merton (1916-1968)

Therefore, I tell you, do not worry about your life, what you will eat or what you will drink, or about your body, what you will wear. Is not life more than food, and the body more than clothing? Look at the birds of the air; they neither sow nor reap nor gather into barns, and yet your heavenly Father feeds them. Are you not of more value than they? And can any of you by worrying add a single hour to your span of life? And why do you worry about clothing? Consider the lilies of the field, how they grow; they neither toil nor spin, yet I tell you, even Solomon in all his glory was not clothed like one of these. But if God so clothes the grass of the field, which is alive today and tomorrow is thrown into the oven, will he not much more clothe you—you of little faith? Therefore, do not worry, saying, "What will we eat?" or "What will we drink?" or "What will we wear?" For it is the Gentiles who strive for all these things; and indeed your heavenly Father knows that you need all these things. But strive first for the kingdom of God and his righteousness, and all these things will be given to you as well. So do not worry about tomorrow, for tomorrow will bring worries of its own. Today's trouble is enough for today.

Jesus in Matthew 6:25-34 (NRSV)

---

6 Thomas Merton, *Conjectures of a Guilty Bystander* (New York: Doubleday, 1966).

Gratitude is a choice. Each one of us chooses every day to what extent we will be grateful—or not. Oxford Languages defines *gratitude* as "the quality of being thankful; readiness to show appreciation for and to return kindness, as in 'She expressed her gratitude to the committee for their support.'"[7]

But come on, who among us does not worry? Who among us never experiences anxiety? It seems to be a requisite of being human. We worry about contracting diseases and illnesses. We worry about the economy and our ability to pay our bills. We worry about our children's safety and their hopes for the future. We worry about crime and our safety. We are filled with anxiety over our divisive politics and dangerous rhetoric in today's society. Yet while some of us are worried about the fate of our democracy, others are mainly concerned about the balance of their 401(k)s. But for the most part, we worry about things we have absolutely no control over.

As Merton stated: "Our anxiety is not imposed on us by forces from outside. We impose it on our world and upon one another from within ourselves."[8]

Researchers say the combination of increased information overload with any ongoing anxiety (such as job stability) can become lethal, producing what some call "toxic worry," which can create mental paralysis.[9]

You and I are living through a period when all the cultural, political, and religious certainties of the past are

---

7 Oxford Languages, s.v. "gratitude," accessed November 24, 2025, https://languages.oup.com/google-dictionary/en/.

8 Thomas Merton, *Conjectures of a Guilty Bystander* (New York: Doubleday, 1966).

9 Kenneth F. Wantland, "'Toxic Worry' Impairs Creativity," *Explorer*, August 1998, https://www.geobyte.com.

unraveling. There is a pervasive feeling that things are out of control. Chaos is the new normal. Needless to say, this is a very unhealthy time of worry and anxiety over COVID-19, job insecurity, economic uncertainty, societal division, and a president who is pressing the boundaries of the executive branch of our government as our place in the world hangs in the balance. Add to that our over-scheduled daily lives, and there you have a perfect recipe for *toxic stress*.

Then there is this: Have you noticed how angry people are these days—from politics and religion to road rage and anger at whoever is not "like me"? And social media has enabled our worst human tendencies with virtually no guardrails.

Yet there is a simple biblical movement that can help us pivot from worry, anxiety, and anger to gratitude. The simple act of gratitude can literally begin to transform our hearts and minds, as well as the way we treat our fellow human beings.

"Don't worry," says Jesus. Easier said than done! Then, in Matthew 6:25, Jesus gets very specific:

- Don't worry about your life.
- Don't worry about your body.
- Don't worry about what you're going to eat or drink.
- And please don't worry about what you're going to wear.

So, here is where we must begin the transformation from worry and anxiety to gratitude—with the honest confession that worry and anxiety are robbing us of our lives. We need to hit the pause button and take time to refocus and reframe our lives. And it all begins with choosing an outlook of gratitude.

Now, please don't misunderstand me: I am not talking about a disingenuous kind of gratitude that ignores the real hurts and losses we share in this human experience, nor of a so-called gratitude that denies the necessity of biblical lament and painful grief over losses that will inevitably come to each of us in this life.

I am also not talking about the terribly destructive theology that permeates modern Christianity with trite sayings like, "Well, everything happens for a reason" or "God needed another angel" in the face of unspeakable tragedy. I am pointing to an indescribable sense of genuine gratitude in the midst of our worst pain, a gratitude in which "deep calls out to deep" as the psalmist writes.

Each year during the last week of November, we gather with people we love to give thanks to God for the blessings that surround us. Sometimes it takes a national holiday to remind us that we should be thankful for all of God's gifts: creation, food, clothing, home, health, friends, family, and faith. But no sooner have we said these things than disturbing questions begin to surface in our minds—not to mention "Black Friday" rolls around the very next day. We wonder to ourselves:

- How will I get everything done this week?
- Why is everything around me changing so rapidly?
- What about my fears of disease and the divisive state of society?

And when will everything finally get back to normal?

Henri Nouwen once suggested that the purest, simplest

holiday may be Thanksgiving. Christmas is distorted by a society that promotes consumer madness. Even Easter's resurrection is overshadowed by innocent chocolate bunnies and spring decorations. But Thanksgiving is about simple gratitude.

It has been said that gratitude is at the very heart of prayer. So, to truly observe Thanksgiving is to be engaged in prayer rather than worry. Yet gratitude cannot be manufactured. It is a gift of grace that God bestows on us and not something we can create in our own hearts. True gratitude bears little resemblance to the forced optimism and "toxic positivity" that underlie phrases such as "count your blessings" or "just grin and bear it."

- Gratitude is not a denial of real pain and loss.
- Gratitude is not a stoic effort to simply concentrate on the good things in life.
- Gratitude is not the "power of positive thinking."
- And we cannot attain a state of gratitude by presenting God with a list of things we think we're supposed to feel grateful for.

Here is where our transformation begins. We become more gracious and generous people as we present ourselves to God with a genuine desire to know God more deeply and grow in our relationship with Him.[10]

"Don't worry," says Jesus. But for some people who claim to follow this same Jesus, their outlook is more like the bumper sticker I once saw that read: "We're born naked, wet, and

---

[10] Kris Haig, "Grateful Hearts," *Presbyterians Today*, November 1999.

hungry. Then things get worse." "Don't worry," says Jesus.

Is Jesus really telling us not to worry about anything? What exactly did Jesus mean as he spoke these words?

Jesus really is telling us not to worry about money, what to eat, or drink, or wear—the basic stuff of life. A large part of Jesus' words here is a lesson in contrasts. And these contrasts are about looking into a completely new reality: the kingdom of God.

For example, when Jesus speaks of not worrying, he points to the birds of the sky and the flowers of the fields. We love to look at fields of flowers in bloom. But the flowers, even in their surpassing beauty, cannot begin to compare with God's greatest creation—humanity itself. This is the true reality: we are all God's children made in his very image, constantly surrounded by God's loving presence.

As for the birds, perhaps there's something we can learn about ourselves from them as well. In their simple lives, they live each day, fully present in each moment as it comes. And living in the "present" with gratitude—rather than in the past or in the future—is one of our greatest challenges.

In a village in the hills of Tanzania, the people of Lulanzi live a simple life. They have a dirt road leading to their village and beyond, and like many similar villages throughout Tanzania, there is no electricity or running water. The people live each day tending their fields, collecting wood for their cooking fires, going to the market, and sending their children to school down the dirt road.

These people of Lulanzi know nothing about the latest

farming equipment. They have no real concept of the internet. They know nothing of MRIs. The people of Lulanzi know a different kind of life—some may call it a better life than those beyond their village. They suffer in times of drought, or when medical problems arise, or when money is scarce for their children's schooling. Yes, sometimes they do worry about life. But they sing!

For the people of Lulanzi, as they gather for worship, as they gather around tables or fields, they sing. They sing songs of God's grace. They sing songs about life. They sing songs about the beauty of God's creation. And their songs are filled with a simple joy that cannot be compared with anything money can buy.[11]

The lives of the people of Lulanzi are so uncomplicated compared to our own hectic lives that they put our lives into perspective. And just maybe, we should all try singing more.

Jesus says, "Do not worry about your life." When we long for a simpler lifestyle, when we're not obsessed with mortgages, bills, kids' schedules, pandemics, international disasters, or elections, we're on our way to less worry.

And perhaps we can hear Jesus' words about not worrying more clearly if we switch our focus to living each day as it comes, just as the birds do, just as the people of Lulanzi do, becoming more grateful and less anxious. So, how do we live the daily grind with gratitude as anxiety-filled Americans?

In Matthew 6:25-34, Jesus sets out eight simple arguments against anxiety:

---

[11] Y. Franklin Ishida, "They Sing," *The Clergy Journal* (Logos Productions).

1. He begins by pointing out in verse 25 that God gave us life, and if God gave us life, surely, we can trust God with the lesser things. So, the first argument is that if God gave us life, we can trust God with the things necessary to sustain it. It's a matter of trusting our Creator.

2. Jesus goes on to speak about the birds in verse 26. There is no worry in their lives, no attempt to pile up goods for an unforeseen and unforeseeable future, and yet their lives go on. The point that Jesus is making is not that the birds do not work. In fact, it has been said that no one works harder than the average sparrow to make a living. The point he is making is that they do not worry. Birds don't get stress-related illnesses.

3. In verse 27, Jesus proves that worry is ultimately useless. This verse can have two meanings. It can mean that by worrying, no one can add a cubit (about 18 inches) to their height. If worrying could do that, then I would be at least 6'7". The verse can also mean that no one can add the shortest space to their life by worrying. Jesus argues that worry is pointless. Worry won't change the outcome of anything.

4. Jesus goes on to speak about the flowers in verses 28-30. They bloomed one day on the hillsides of Palestine, and yet in their brief life, they were clothed with a beauty that surpassed the beauty of the kings' robes. When the flowers died, they were used for nothing better than burning.

5. A first-century Palestinian oven was made of clay, like a clay box set on bricks over the fire. If someone wanted to raise the temperature very quickly, they would fling handfuls of dried grass and wildflowers into the oven and set them on fire. So, the point is, the flowers had only one day of life, and then they were set on fire. So, if God gives such beauty to a short-lived flower, how much more will he care for his people?

6. Jesus goes on to advance a very fundamental argument against worry in verse 32. Worry, he says, is characteristic of a heathen, not of those who trust in the love and provision of their Heavenly Father.

7. Next, Jesus states how we are to defeat worry in verse 33. Seek first—focus upon—the kingdom of God. Concentrating on doing and accepting God's will is the way to defeat worry. It was Jesus' conviction that worry is banished when God becomes the dominating power of our lives.

8. Finally, Jesus says that worry can be defeated when we learn the art of living one day at a time (v. 34). The Jewish people had a saying: "Do not worry over tomorrow's evils, for you know not what today will bring forth. Perhaps tomorrow you will not be alive, and you will have worried for a world which will not be yours."

Jesus tells us to handle the demands of each day as they come, without worrying about the unknown future and the things that may never even happen.

I want to close this meditation with two stories about the transformative process of becoming more grateful and less anxious. I don't know if they actually happened, but I do know they are true!

Once there was a rich businessman who was disturbed to find a fisherman sitting lazily beside his boat. He asked the fisherman, "Why aren't you out there fishing?" "Because I've caught enough fish for today," said the fisherman. "Well, why don't you catch more fish than you need?" the rich man asked.

"Well, what would I do with them?" came the reply.

"You could earn more money and buy a better boat so you could go deeper and catch more fish. You could purchase nylon nets, catch even more fish, and make more money. Soon you'd have a fleet of boats and be rich like me."

The fisherman asked, "Then what would I do?" "You could sit down and enjoy life," said the businessman. The fisherman replied, "What do you think I'm doing now?"[12]

The second story is set early in the twentieth century. An American tourist traveled to Poland to visit a famous rabbi. Noticing that his room only had a table, a chair, and some books, the American asked, "Rabbi, where is your furniture?"

The rabbi replied, "My furniture? Where is your furniture, my friend?" "But I am only a tourist, passing through," said the American. To which the rabbi replied: "So am I."[13]

Remember these words of Jesus: "Don't worry about your life ... BUT seek first the kingdom of God." It's that simple and that difficult. But if you will repeat these words every day as a prayer of surrender and thanksgiving to God, then the transformation begins.

---

[12] "The Contented Fisherman," *Preaching Today,* accessed November 24, 2025, https://www.preachingtoday.com/illustrations/1998/february/3605.html.

[13] Alan Smith, "Just Passing Through," SermonIllustrator.org, accessed November 24, 2025, https://www.sermonillustrator.org/illustrator/sermon14/just_passing_through.htm.

It starts with the simple act of gratitude, and then we find that we are sustained daily by having a grateful heart. So, I invite you to intentionally cultivate more gratitude during these anxious times in which we live.

We've tried arguing and complaining, and see where that's gotten us! After all, what have we got to lose—except maybe a little stress, worry, and anxiety?

Reflection and Action

1. Do you think that a person can be filled with anxiety and gratitude at the same time?

2. What is one thing you can do this week to lessen your anxiety?

3. How does gratitude gradually overcome worry?

4. In what ways can your congregation help people become less anxious and more grateful?

CHAPTER THREE

Living the Daily Grind with Gratitude

Praise the Lord! O give thanks to the Lord, for he is good; for his steadfast love endures forever. Who can utter the mighty doings of the Lord, or declare all his praise? Happy are those who observe justice, who do righteousness at all times.

Psalm 106:1-3 (NRSV)

If we really want to improve our lives, our congregations, and our communities:

- Is it more effective to reduce negativity or increase positivity?
- Does it help most if we cultivate a more positive environment or a less negative one?
- Which action is more effective?

In her article "Less Negative Beats more Positive," Dr. Julia A. West answers these questions:

> *As it turns out, working to reduce negativity has a ripple effect that outweighs trying to add positivity into your life. In 2021, a team of researchers led by Michael F. Scheier conducted a meta-analysis of sixty-one studies. Findings across these studies demonstrated that less pessimism was a more powerful predictor of better physical health outcomes than more optimism.*[14]

---

[14] Julia A. West, "Less Negative Beats More Positive," *Limitless Minds*, accessed November 24, 2025, https://limitlessminds.com/less-negative-beats-more-positive/?v=92a31fc033f7.

So, if you want to improve your environment—and your physical and mental health in the process—identifying current patterns of negativity and reducing them is a great place to start. West continues:

> *Here is what their definition of negativity doesn't include:*
>
> - *Challenging feedback or asking the hard questions*
> - *Raising concerns or reaching out for support or help*
> - *Identifying a problem and wanting to process it with the goal of finding a solution with your colleagues.*
> - *These are all examples of necessary behaviors in high-performing teams. (Just because something isn't what you "want" to hear doesn't mean that it's negative!) Sometimes, it's just an accurate description of the objective truth!*[15]

Author and professor Adam Grant (@AdamMGrant) sums this up:

> *Optimism has little bearing on health. Avoiding pessimism has more. Sixty-one studies, with 221,000 people: Health is predicted more by the absence of pessimism than the presence of optimism. Well-being isn't about expecting the best. It's about making sure you don't assume the worst.*[16]

While many choose to combat negativity by piling on positivity, there's actually a more efficient way to go about it: addition by subtraction—lose the negative complaining, fault-finding, over-generalizing, and catastrophizing. You don't have to become one of those toxic-positivity people who ignores the truth and the hard realities of life; you just have to reduce the unhelpful constant flow of negativity.

---

[15] West, "Less Negative."

[16] West, "Less Negative."

Researchers also tell us that having a grateful heart is good for you, and many studies confirm that gratitude actually has mental and physical benefits. But there's a catch: you must be grateful more than just once a year.

- Case in point, if you post a list of the things you are thankful for on Facebook for one week in November, but you're a complainer the other fifty-one weeks of the year, then it's probably best to keep that gratitude list to yourself.
- If you go to the gym once a year, what good is that really doing for your body?
- If you go to school once a year, what good is that really doing for your education?
- Or if you go to church once a year, what good is that really doing for your spiritual growth? You get the picture.

A simple act of gratitude woven into the fabric of our daily practices can transform our lives and the way we treat our fellow human beings. A little dose of gratitude is that powerful! So, what should motivate us to live with gratitude every day, at all times?

It is not a denial of pain, evil, or injustice. At the end of the day, it is all about choosing gratitude as your default setting because no one knows what tomorrow will bring.

The following story comes directly from my friend and church member, Larry Swanda, in his own words. I had the privilege of baptizing Larry, and I share his story with his permission.

In the early 2000s, I was working at Smithfield Foods and also had a swine production unit that I operated with my former wife. From time to time, we needed additional help for the operation. I had been working with a neighbor, Jim, on some farming projects, and he asked if we needed help and could his son, Dan, work on the farm? It was a good opportunity for both of us. Dan did a variety of things, from feeding animals, washing aisles, to vaccinating animals.

After my wife and I separated, I was depressed and self-isolated, not doing any activities other than going to work and running the hog farm. Dan became very helpful in checking and working the farm because I was extremely busy. At work, my close friends were very supportive and suggested that I should go to church. One Sunday morning, I decided I would get dressed and go to Mount Olive and find a church to attend. I drove by a couple of churches and stopped at the First Baptist. I went in and sat at the back near the door.

I attended the church for several Sundays and became friends with a nice lady who was welcoming and encouraging. One Sunday, there was a service that would become very special and unforgettable. On that Sunday, these four words were spoken, "In everything give thanks."

On a Saturday afternoon, a week or two later, around 2:30 or 3 p.m., Jim came by to see if I would mind if he helped my wife move her belongings out of the house. I told him it would be fine for him to help move her belongings. He asked how I was doing. I replied that things were getting better and that I had started to attend church at First Baptist. I told him that one Sunday service was special to me. I told him, "In everything give thanks." He said, "Well, I guess now you can be thankful that you will have more time to deer hunt." We both laughed.

I had become friends with a lady named Kim who had her Ph.D. in clinical psychology. She was a very smart and charming person who was supportive, inspiring, and worked with her patients from a Christian perspective.

That night, I had returned from a dinner engagement and was getting ready to retire. It was about 11:30 p.m. when I heard sirens east of the house. I did not think a great deal about it at the time.

Around 7:30 a.m. the next morning, I awoke to a knock on the kitchen door. I looked out, and it was Dan's sister. Inviting her in, I noticed she was very distressed. She came to tell me about an accident in which someone had been killed. Still half asleep, I asked her to repeat who was killed. She said it was Dan. I remember saying, "Oh no, not Dan." He had died in a head-on crash a mile from the house that night. After collecting my thoughts and expressing sorrow, she asked if I would be a pallbearer at the funeral. I said it would be an honor to do so.

A few days later, I attended the wake for Dan. In the receiving line, I exchanged sympathies with family members. When I spoke to Dan's father, he told me that when he saw his son's body in the crashed car, he thought of these words: "In everything give thanks." He was thankful the car did not catch fire so he could see his son once more for the last time. I thought about that night many times, and I believed that God used me to help prepare Dan's father for that night.

Later that same year, Kim and I attended a Christmas event with some friends. Dan's parents were also at the event. Dan's mother talked about her son and talked about Dan being a typical teenager who loved to play around with BBs. Sometime after Dan had passed away, Dan's mother had cleaned off the kitchen table to get ready for Sunday supper. The table was set, and food was placed in the center. Getting ready to eat, Dan's mother picked up her napkin—and there was a BB under it. She asked, "Who placed the BB under my napkin?" Silence. No one answered. How did the BB end up under the napkin on a table that had just been completely cleaned off? One of God's "Mysterious Ways" to send reassurance to a grieving mother?

Around this time, Kim was counseling another woman who had also lost her son. The bereaved mother had been diagnosed with terminal cancer, and knowing her time was short, was earnestly searching for reassurance that her son had gone to heaven. Kim counseled from a Christian perspective and thought it may be helpful to tell her about Dan and the BB incident. Kim shared the story with her counselee as a gentle reminder of God's continued love and care even in times of deep sorrow and grief. The woman listened to the BB story.

Sometime later, she returned to Kim's office and told Kim she had received a sign that her son had gone to heaven. The BB story helped lift the burden of doubt from her heart.

On the same night that Dan died, his eighteen-year-old friend also died in that accident with him. Dan's friend was the son of a pastor. Three sons, three grieving families. One ever-present God who is always with us and sometimes speaks to us in unusual ways.

Larry's story provides a witness to the power of the simple daily practice of gratitude. Over and over, the psalmist instructs God's people, "Give thanks to the Lord, for he is good; his steadfast love endures forever"(Psalm 106:1, NIV). And regardless of our individual experiences or personal benefits, the Bible calls us collectively—as the people of God—to continually give thanks to God together, transforming our occasional expressions of thanks into living gratefully and consistently as a community of faith.

So, choosing to live with gratitude in the daily grind is more than making a list of things we're thankful for—it is a way of being, of living consistently. Living gratefully involves making a deliberate choice. As a result, you can live each day striving to love God with all your being and love all your neighbors even as you love yourself.

Psalm 106:3 says: "Happy are those who observe justice, who do righteousness at all times." But some people seem miserable "at all times," and they want others to come and join them. After all, misery does love company.

I recently came across a snarky little article entitled "14 Habits of Highly Miserable People," written by Cloe Madanes. It describes the very opposite way of living with gratitude. In the article, Madanes lists fourteen ways to cultivate a life of misery. So, just in case you're interested, here are fourteen ways that you, or someone you know, can cultivate a life of misery:

1. **Be afraid of economic loss.** Concentrate on this fear and make it a priority in your life. Complain continuously that you could go broke any day and about how much everything costs.

2. **Practice sustained boredom.** Cultivate the feeling that everything is predictable, that life holds no excitement, no possibility for adventure. Also, complain a lot about how bored you are.

3. **Give yourself a negative identity.** Allow a perceived emotional problem to absorb all other aspects of your self-identity. If you suffer from social anxiety or a phobia, assume the identity of phobia or anxiety and make your condition the focus of your life!

4. **Pick fights.** This is an excellent way of ruining a relationship with a romantic partner or friend. Once in a while, unpredictably pick a fight or have a crying spell over something trivial and make unwarranted accusations. The interaction should last for at least 15 minutes and ideally occur in public.

5. **Attribute bad intentions.** Whenever you can, attribute the worst possible intentions to your partner, friends, and coworkers. Take any innocent remark and turn it into an insult or attempt to humiliate you personally.

6. **Whatever you do, do it only for personal gain.** Sometimes you'll be tempted to help someone, contribute to a charity, or participate in a community activity. Don't do it, unless there's something in it for you.

7. **Avoid gratitude.** Research shows that people who express gratitude are happier than those who don't, so never express gratitude. Counting your blessings is for losers. What blessings? Life is suffering, and then you die.

8. **Always be alert and in a state of anxiety.** Optimism about the future only leads to disappointment. Therefore, you must believe that ... nothing good will ever work out for you. Also ... do some research on what disasters could occur in your area, such as earthquakes, hurricanes, floods, nuclear plant leaks & rabies outbreaks. Focus on these things for at least an hour a day.

9. **Blame your parents.** Blaming your parents for your defects, shortcomings, and failures is among the most important steps you can take. After all, your parents made you who you are today; YOU had nothing to do with it.

10. **Don't enjoy life's pleasures.** Taking pleasure in things like food, nature, music, and beauty is for shallow people. Constantly remind yourself that the world is full of poverty, illness & devastation. The beauty of nature is a deception.

11. **Ruminate.** Spend a great deal of time focused on yourself. Worry constantly about the causes of your behavior, analyze your defects, and chew on your problems. This will help foster a pessimistic view of your life.

12. **Glorify or vilify the past.** Glorifying the past is telling yourself how good, happy, and worthwhile life WAS when you were younger—and regretting how it's all been downhill ever since. Vilifying the past means you were born in the wrong place at the wrong time. How can you be happy when you have such a lousy background?

13. **(If you are single) find a romantic partner to reform.** Make sure that you fall in love with someone who has a major defect (e.g., a cat hoarder, gambler, alcoholic, womanizer, or sociopath), and set out to reform him or her, regardless of whether he or she wants to be reformed. Believe firmly that only you can reform this person and ignore all evidence to the contrary. (We used to call that "missionary dating!") AND FINALLY...

14. **Be critical.** Make sure to have an endless list of dislikes and voice them often, even if your opinion isn't solicited. For example, don't hesitate to say, "That's what you chose to wear this morning?" or "Why is your voice so annoying?" If someone is eating eggs, simply tell them you don't like eggs. Your negativity can be applied to almost any situation![17]

These fourteen habits should, in a practical way, help you cultivate a life of misery. But if you would rather live with gratitude, then do the very opposite of these fourteen habits.

We tend to think that our joy and happiness depend on our personality type, our DNA, the circumstances we face, or how much money we have in the bank. But the psalmist says it has to do with giving thanks to God AND doing justice and

---

[17] Cloe Madanes, "14 Habits of Highly Miserable People," *The Huffington Post,* accessed November 24, 2025, https://www.huffpost.com/entry/14-habits-of-highly-mis_b_6397528.

righteousness as a way of living—all the time.

Among the many biblical passages that call us to live each day with gratitude, the apostle Paul offers this instruction to the Thessalonians: "Give thanks in all circumstances; for this is the will of God in Christ Jesus for you" (1 Thess. 5:18, NRSV).

But you may be thinking, "Those folks didn't have to face what we do today." They didn't have to deal with a global pandemic; they didn't have to deal with division and racism; they didn't have to deal with rising debt and unemployment, or a society that is losing its moral compass; they didn't have to deal with global warming, terrorism, the decline of democracy, and the approaching apocalyptic doom.

Actually, these Thessalonian Christians believed they were the ones living in the Last Days two thousand years ago. They faced persecution and poverty, disease, and misery with the boot of the Roman Empire on their necks. And they wanted it all to go away. They wanted Jesus to return.

That's why Paul reminds the Thessalonians that "the day of the Lord will come like a thief in the night," and because we do not know when, he urges believers to "rejoice always, pray without ceasing, and give thanks in all circumstances; for this is the will of God in Christ Jesus for you" (1 Thess. 5:2, 16–18, NRSV).

The question for us, two thousand years later, is this: how can we pivot from being grateful only occasionally to living with gratitude every day? For followers of Jesus, three truths enable this shift:

1. **Living the daily grind with gratitude flows from a relationship with God Almighty.** First and

foremost, genuine Christian gratitude flows from a dynamic relationship with God. Throughout the Bible, every declaration of gratitude can be traced to that person's relationship with God. We cannot live a life of gratitude without first connecting to the Source of love and grace and remaining connected. Jesus says: "I am the vine; you are the branches;" apart from me, you can do nothing. So, gratitude first arises out of a growing, dynamic relationship with God through Christ. It's the kind of genuine gratitude that persists even on bad days, even when we are facing major difficulties, even when we're lying flat on our backs. An attitude of gratitude to God flows out of the joy of this relationship, rather than in response to the situations we confront. The psalmist proclaims: "The Lord is good ... his steadfast love endures forever"—meaning God can be trusted. God is not mad at you or out to get you. God is good! As simple, or as basic as it may sound, genuine Christian gratitude first flows from a deepening relationship with God our Creator—who is always good, always loving, and always faithful.

2. **Living the daily grind with gratitude is an act of faith.** You can hear this in Paul's words to the Romans in Chapter 5:3-4: "We also boast in our sufferings, knowing that suffering produces endurance, and endurance produces character, and character produces hope, and hope does not disappoint us" (NRSV). But if you're like me, sometimes you find yourself thinking: "Um, Lord, I'm working on more character than I'll ever need for one lifetime." But based on everything I have seen, heard, and experienced myself, I think Paul was right. If you pay attention, the best-lived lives seem to develop on the OTHER side of suffering. It is in the daily grind that I find myself getting frustrated, angry, and

tempted to complain. I can't just pop up and do things the way I used to—or at least not as quickly. Living in the daily grind requires us "perfectionists" to allow ourselves some grace, just as we should be willing to give grace to others. I don't wish suffering on anyone or seek it for myself. But I am leery of anyone who has never suffered or at least been honest about the questions of suffering. Because when you honestly think about it, the ability to experience genuine gratitude for any kind of difficulty is almost always done in retrospect—looking back. So, that makes being grateful in the midst of that difficulty a subversive act of faith. It is a form of resistance to the status quo. We know that God is not the author of our pain; therefore, it is always an act of faith in God's goodness and ability to bring something good out of our pain. We all have our own kinds of suffering, and because of those times, we know firsthand that living with gratitude is, at its core, an act of defiance and faith.

3. **Living the daily grind with gratitude is expressed in giving.** Christian thanksgiving is ultimately expressed in giving to others. The opposite of this is the picture of a person whose hands are tightly wrapped around their personal possessions and time while mouthing praise to God. The poster child for false gratitude is the Pharisee Jesus talked about who stood in the temple and prayed: "God, I thank you that I am not like all those other people—thieves, rogues, adulterers, or even like this tax collector. I fast twice a week; I give a tenth of all my income" (Luke 18:11-12, NRSV). The only thing this guy was grateful for was NOT being like those "less fortunate people." The posture of genuine gratitude includes arms and hands open and outstretched—sharing what we have, inviting people to the table, offering a warm coat or a kind

word, and demonstrating compassion toward others. This is living with gratitude as the way of life that lasts fifty-two weeks a year. If we ever hope to move from occasional thanksgiving to living with gratitude daily, then we will also need to learn to be impatient when people in need are NOT being served and are being excluded. As verse 3 tells us: "Happy are those who observe justice, who do righteousness at ALL TIMES" (Psalm 106:3, NRSV). This is gratitude in action. Living with gratitude must always be expressed in loving action to others: doing the right, kind, and loving thing at all times.

4. **But can we really offer gratitude to God when so much is wrong in our world today?** We can if we remember that living gratefully flows from a relationship with God and is a defiant act of faith ultimately expressed in giving to others.

If you strip away all our differences, maybe there are only two kinds of people in this world: those who complain and those who are grateful. Where are you on this continuum? A chronic complainer? Or someone filled with gratitude?

Where you are located on this continuum will directly correlate with your level of joy and peace. Complain OR live each day with gratitude. For those who live with gratitude, "happily observe justice and do righteousness" at all times.

You can be a chronic complainer, or you can live your life with gratitude and work for justice. It's a daily choice we all make.

Consider the full version of the familiar "Serenity Prayer," written by Reinhold Niebuhr, as your prayer for living the daily grind with gratitude:

God, grant me the serenity
To accept the things I cannot change,
Courage to change the things I can,
And wisdom to know the difference.
Living one day at a time;
Enjoying one moment at a time;
Accepting hardship as the pathway to peace.
Taking, as He did, this sinful world as it is,
not as I would have it.
Trusting that He will make all things right
if I surrender to His Will.
That I may be reasonably happy in this life,
And supremely happy with Him forever in the next.

Amen.

Reflection and Action

1. How do you respond to Larry's story of "giving thanks in all circumstances"?

2. Does daily gratitude come easily for you, or is it difficult to express?

3. What can you resolve to do that will help you cultivate living with MORE gratitude daily?

4. Name some concrete ways that your gratitude can move you to work for justice on behalf of others. Who are the "others" in your own community?

5. Read the "Serenity Prayer" out loud. What words or phrases really connect with your life? What does it mean for you to live "reasonably happy?"

CHAPTER FOUR

The Movements of Gratitude

Now when Jesus heard this, he withdrew from there in a boat to a deserted place by himself. But when the crowds heard it, they followed him on foot from the towns. When he went ashore, he saw a great crowd, and he had compassion for them and cured their sick. When it was evening, the disciples came to him and said, "This is a deserted place, and the hour is now late; send the crowds away so that they may go into the villages and buy food for themselves." Jesus said to them, "They need not go away; you give them something to eat." They replied, "We have nothing here but five loaves and two fish." And he said, "Bring them here to me." Then he ordered the crowds to sit down on the grass. Taking the five loaves and the two fish, he looked up to heaven and blessed and broke the loaves and gave them to the disciples, and the disciples gave them to the crowds. And all ate and were filled, and they took up what was left over of the broken pieces, twelve baskets full. And those who ate were about five thousand men, besides women and children.

Matthew 14:13-21 (NRSV)

Over the years of raising three boys within a family of five, mealtimes were often a challenge:

- challenging to find something that everybody would eat and enjoy
- challenging to find a time when everyone could be present and sit down together
- challenging to truly be thankful for whatever was on the menu

There is always a great temptation among us in modern America to take food for granted and not be fully present with one another around the tables where we gather, especially amid the distractions, busyness, and technology that engulf us.

But in first-century Jewish culture, eating a meal was more of an event shared together than it was simply gobbling down fast food on the run. Meals were about hospitality and sharing in the community. If you ate with someone, it meant you were investing in building that relationship, something Jesus showed was very important to him.

In fact, if you take a quick survey of the Gospels, you will find that Jesus loved to practice two things consistently: healing and eating with others. Jesus healed many people, and he also went around dining with a wide range of people—from religious elites to the outcasts of society.

For Jesus, eating with people from all sides of life's spectrum was a tangible sign of things to come and was very much connected to his mission of proclaiming God's kingdom. He was acting out the principle that the kingdom of God is an inclusive reality where everyone is welcomed, and everyone gets their fair share of the best food. For Jesus, this was not a theoretical concept or simply a good idea; it was a lived-out reality.

Even with all the Jewish dietary restrictions, the main objection by his opponents wasn't about what Jesus ate but who Jesus ate with. Seated at tables is where Jesus finds much trouble from his critics because of who he intentionally sat down with for hospitality and food.

When we hear the familiar story of Jesus feeding the 5,000-

plus, we are reminded that the hungry are always with us—people hungry for their next meal, hungry for God, hungry for grace and forgiveness, hungry for community and a chance to find meaning for their lives.

Then we can hear Jesus turn to his disciples and say, "You give them something to eat." And we see that whatever small portion we may have to offer becomes great when placed in the hands of Jesus. So, rather than throwing up our hands in frustration when faced with the enormous needs around us, Jesus invites us to take inventory, to take stock—not of what we don't have but of what we do have to offer. And we have a lot more than we think we do. It's here in this story that we find the basic pattern for living with gratitude as Christ-followers today.

When we share the bread and juice, protestants mostly know this as The Lord's Supper, or Holy Communion. But many other Christians around the world know this experience as Eucharist, the Greek word meaning "the giving of thanks, or gratitude."

In the New Testament, two terms are associated with the Lord's Supper: *eucharist`eo,* or "thanksgiving," is used, as is *eulog`eo,* meaning "to bless." Whether you call it Holy Communion, the Eucharist, or the Lord's Supper, we celebrate this meal in remembrance of Jesus Christ, commemorating the last meal with his disciples and his sacrifice for the forgiveness of sins.

Something we may tend to miss at the center of the communion meal is an attitude and spirit of thanksgiving for the life and sacrifice of Jesus. Eucharist! And through the miracle of feeding the 5,000 (plus women and children), we are given a model for how we ought to live with gratitude every day.

In practical terms, a eucharistic way of life follows five basic movements, as Jesus exemplifies—blessing, breaking, receiving, giving, and going. The five movements provide us with a model for Christian living at all times—with gratitude. This is the eucharistic way of gratitude:

1. **BLESSING:** Blessing is the act of naming God's presence in all that we do. Jesus raised the bread to heaven and gave thanks—or invoked God's blessing upon the food before he attempted to distribute it. To invoke God's name in our daily lives is to recognize God's presence that is already there. In this act of blessing, we look for the sacred in the simple events that run through our lives. All times have the potential to reveal "God with us" as we name and discover God's presence. So, as we take bread, we give thanks for it so we may be open to encountering God as we gather around the table with others. We begin to live a eucharistic way of life with the act of blessing.

2. **BREAKING:** This may be the most difficult of these practices. In one sense, breaking is simply the act of dividing what we have to share with those around us. It is rooted in the vision of the early Christian community in Acts 2, which shared all things in common and distributed to anyone in need. Sometimes the hardest thing for us is letting go and sharing freely with others. But in another sense, breaking bread symbolically acknowledges the brokenness of our own lives and our need for God's healing. If we are honest, then we must admit that we are all broken, flawed human beings. Our own brokenness is rooted in Christ's brokenness on the cross, which paves the way for God's work of resurrection. Paul wrote:

But he said to me, "My grace is sufficient for you, for power is made perfect in weakness." So, I will boast all the more gladly of my weaknesses, so that the power of Christ may dwell in me. Therefore I am content with weaknesses, insults, hardships, persecutions, and calamities for the sake of Christ; for whenever I am weak, then I am strong."

2 Corinthians 12:9 (NRSV)

So, we are blessed as we humbly admit that we are broken.

3. **RECEIVING:** In a world driven by consumption and greed, the concept of receiving can be misconstrued as an excuse to grab whatever we want. In a time when there is an ever-growing gap between "the haves and the have-nots," taking whatever we want at the expense of others is often justified. But at the table, instead of taking as much as we want, we are taught gratitude through the humble act of receiving. In the feeding of the 5,000-plus, the act of Jesus receiving bread from the little boy is rooted in an act of generosity—a young boy offers his lunch and, by the presence of God, provides enough for everyone to eat until they are full. Jesus accepts, or receives, what is offered to him. In a similar way, we practice receiving with gratitude whatever is handed to us as a sign of God's faithfulness. So, we bless and are broken, and we learn to receive the gifts of God's grace. Through seemingly insignificant gifts, God does miraculous things!

4. **GIVING:** We bless, we break, we humbly receive, but in following the pattern of Christ, we must move to the act of giving. As we respond to the invitation to the table, we find our lives reshaped in the example of Christ. As we allow these movements to shape and form our lives, we become more thankful and more generous people. Just as Christ gave his life for the forgiveness of sins—and just as a young boy gave a meager offering of bread and fish—we are called to

give whatever we have to the glory of God. And the point is not how much we have to give but that we give whatever we have.

5. **GOING.** A eucharistic life of gratitude culminates in reminding us that, as Letty Russell puts it, "Our mission flows from this meal." As we bless, and break, and receive, and give, we must finally go into the world. "Just as the Father has sent me, so I send you," said Jesus. We give thanks that God sent his Son, and then we go into the world and allow this gospel to be made known through our words and actions. The model of Jesus reminds us that we are to go out into the world, allowing ourselves to be broken and poured out for the sake of others, following in the example of our Lord.[18]

So, these five movements of gratitude have the power to form a eucharistic way of living in us—blessing, breaking, receiving, giving, and going. Each one of these is offered to God with thanksgiving and hope. Within each movement, we act in faith that God will multiply the gifts we bring for God's reign of peace and justice to take hold in the world. Even in the face of death, we cling to the promise and hope of resurrection.

Just as Jesus loved to eat meals with friends and strangers, most churches are pretty good at eating together, too. So, as we gather, let's gather expectantly and remember the five movements of the eucharistic life of gratitude.

These five movements serve as a template for living with gratitude at all times by:

---

[18] Alban Institute, "Eucharist as a Way of Life," May 1, 2008, accessed November 24, 2025, https://alban.org/archive/eucharist-as-a-way-of-life/. Adapted from Paul Galbreath, *Leading from the Table* (Rowman & Littlefield, 2008).

- Cultivating a grateful heart.
- Humbling ourselves continuously.
- Forgiving our neighbors.
- Depending on God's provision.
- Welcoming strangers.
- Practicing hospitality.
- Sharing our belongings.
- Recognizing Christ's presence.
- Caring for all of God's creation.
- And learning to let go of power and control.

If we humbly break bread with those with whom we disagree, our differences might begin to be set aside in light of the act of giving thanks.

The Masai tribe in East Africa has a rather unusual model for saying "thank you." They say, "My head is in the dirt." When the Masai express thanks, they literally put their foreheads to the ground to acknowledge their gratitude with humility.

Another African tribe expresses gratitude by saying, "I sit on the ground before you."

If one of them wants to express gratitude to another, he goes to the house of the person to whom he wants to express gratitude—and he just sits there in front of the house in humility for an extended length of time.[19]

The eucharistic way of life Jesus models in this miraculous story moves from blessing and breaking to receiving, giving,

[19] Joel Gregory, "The Unlikely Thanker," *Preaching Today,* tape no. 110.

and going. May we allow these movements to work their way into our daily living. If we do, then we will embody Paul's prayer in Colossians 3:17: "And whatever you do, in word or deed, do everything in the name of the Lord Jesus, giving thanks to God" (NRSV). May it be so in us.

REFLECTION & ACTION

1. How wide and inclusive are the tables around which you gather? What about the tables around which your congregation gathers?

2. What is one thing you can do to widen the tables around which you gather daily, weekly, monthly, and yearly?

3. Of the five movements of gratitude, which one do you struggle with the most?

4. Which one are you most comfortable with? What about your congregation?

Von Ao 1617
Bis Ao 1650
Catechismus
M. Mart. Rinkart.
Archidiac. geb. zu Eilenburg 1580

CHAPTER FIVE
A Heart of Gratitude

I give you thanks, O Lord with my whole heart;
before the gods I sing your praise;
I bow down toward your holy temple
and give thanks to your name for your steadfast love and your faithfulness,
for you have exalted your name and your word above everything.
On the day I called, you answered me;
you increased my strength of soul.

For though the Lord is high, he regards the lowly,
but the haughty he perceives from far away.

Psalm 138:1-3, 6 (NRSV)

Did you know that nearly 80 percent of Americans say they feel deep gratitude at least once a week? Sounds to me like some generous self-reporting based on what we would like to imagine is the case. If this were really true, wouldn't that deep gratitude translate into a more grateful society? Honestly, do you have a grateful heart? On some days, maybe. But on other days, not so much.

And did you know that recognizing and giving thanks for the positive aspects of life can result in improved mental, and ultimately physical health? In a study of patients with asymptomatic heart failure, gratitude can be a healing force, according to research published by the American Psychological Association.

"We found that more gratitude in these patients was associated with better mood, better sleep, less fatigue and lower levels of inflammatory biomarkers related to cardiac health," says lead author Paul J. Mills, PhD, professor of family medicine and public health at the University of California, San Diego.[20]

So, a grateful person also has a stronger, healthier heart—physically. But how can we cultivate a more grateful heart spiritually? For starters, the writer of Psalm 138 begins, "I give you thanks, O LORD, with my whole heart" (NRSV).

Most of us are aware that we should be coming before the one true God with thanksgiving. But what about with your "whole heart"? Do we really do anything wholeheartedly these days?

Our hearts are divided by busyness, social media, work, career ambition, activities, and more. I know young families who seem wholeheartedly committed to year-round youth baseball, soccer, or a dozen other sports. They have convinced themselves that this sport is the most important factor in developing their future professional athlete, and they can't afford to have their child left behind.

I've been there as well, and I understand the temptation to believe that your child's sport deserves your whole heart. But that belief must be kept in perspective—much of it is a false illusion.

What, or whom, is truly worthy of your whole heart? Your list should be very short. Think about that question before

---

[20] Paul J. Mills et al., "The Role of Gratitude in Spiritual Well-Being in Asymptomatic Heart Failure Patients," *Spirituality in Clinical Practice 2, no. 1* (2015), accessed December 8, 2025, https://doi.org/10.1037/scp0000050.

you allow your heart to be divided among lesser gods. The psalmist writes:

> *I give you thanks, O Lord, with my whole heart;*
> *before the gods I sing your praise.*

Across our country, fewer worshipers are making their way to churches to "come into God's presence with thanksgiving." The causes are multi-layered and have been permeating among us for decades—and it is happening everywhere.

Be that as it may, giving thanks has always been one of the most central acts of worship for the people of God. However, the institutional church has, in many cases, lost its way in the 21st century. Of course, this did not happen overnight. It has been coming for decades. Christian nationalism, ethical scandals, devotion to tradition, and selling out to pop culture are among the culprits.

Someone once said, "Jesus came preaching the kingdom of God, and we created the church." But the kingdom of God is still coming all around us. Take a look around your community and discover where God is at work.

I believe God is reshaping the church today because our hearts have become deeply divided, and gratitude is one of the simplest ways for us to return to our true home. God will always have "a people," no matter what happens to the church. Many also long for the transformation of the institutional church. So, do not lose heart, come before God with your whole heart, and trust in his goodness to always provide a way. Our God is above all other gods.

However, we often live out of a mindset of scarcity rather

than the abundance of the God of all Creation. When that happens, we become blind to our blessings. So many people today have come to see the good things of life as something meant to be guarded and hoarded rather than a gift to be shared. And when that happens, we lose the sense of wonder and surprise that gives birth to true gratitude.

John Sandel, the host and founder of the podcast and website Stoic Coffee Break, says, "When we recognize that we are being given a gift ... we feel joy ... and gratitude is the experience that flows from this joy."[21] It often starts with young children, who are showered with presents by their parents so that the gifts they receive at holidays and birthdays are not recognized as gifts but instead as their "just payment due."

But of course, children aren't the only ones who get caught in this trap. Teenagers and adults use their earnings to load up on the latest technology, clothing, and cars in pursuit of a level of prosperity that previous generations took decades to achieve. This mindset breeds a sense of entitlement. We buy into the unrealistic illusion that "bad things" aren't supposed to ever happen to me. We create unrealistic notions about happiness—as if happiness is all that matters.

This ancient psalm (Psalm 138) is meant to cultivate grateful hearts among the people of God in every time and place because of God's "steadfast love" *(hesed)* and "faithfulness" *(emeth)*. And ultimately, this gratitude culminates in acts of

---

[21] Henry G. Brinton, "Here is the Church. Where Are the People?" *The Washington Post*, November 18, 2000.

love, service, and compassion with the most vulnerable people in society because God regards the lowly, but the haughty he perceives from far away (Psalm 138:6).

Therefore, true gratitude always leads to acts of service, love, and compassion to those whom God regards as lowly rather than those who think too highly of themselves.

For some, it takes our government declaring a national holiday to remind us to give thanks at least once a year. But the reality for Christians is that every day is a day of praise and thanksgiving to God—in the good times, in the ordinary times, and even in the worst of times.

In 1636, during the Thirty Years' War—one of the worst wars in the history of humankind—there was a godly pastor named Martin Rinkart. In a single year, this pastor buried 5,000 people in his parish, about fifteen every day. He lived with the worst that life could offer.

In the middle of that horrible time, Martin Rinkart wrote a prayer of table grace for his children, which is now sung as the hymn "Now Thank We All Our God":

Now thank we all our God.
With hearts and hands and voices,
Who wondrous things has done,
In whom his world rejoices.

Giving praise and thanks to God is a regular, weekly act of our worship as the church and a continuous, daily act for each Christian. Thanksgiving has been infused into our spiritual DNA as the people of God since the Exodus, and we are still called upon today to respond to God with a spirit of gratitude in our hearts, on our lips, and ultimately through our actions.

Without thanksgiving and praise, we are like corpses in a cathedral. But with each moment of giving praise and thanks to God, we discover that God breathes life and energy back into us, compelling us to show our gratitude to God by serving others. True gratitude always leads to acts of love, service, and compassion.

The lack of a grateful heart results in a hardened heart, as the ancestors of Israel experienced in the wilderness. Either we cultivate a grateful heart, OR we will suffer from many "heart failures." But let's not overcomplicate or overthink gratitude.

Meister Eckhart, a German mystic and philosopher (1260-1328), is attributed with saying very simply that if the only prayer you ever say in your life is "thank you," it will be enough. How is that possible? Because God looks at the heart.

You may not be connected to a local church at all for a variety of reasons, and that is okay. I get it. Church has not been a happy or healthy experience for many, going back to their childhood or teenage years. But God is not bound by the walls of a church building.

What are the greatest unmet needs in your community? What people are falling through cracks in the social service systems and churches in your area? What needs are hidden from the average divided heart? Grab some friends and do good in your community.

We can all cultivate gratitude by coming expectantly into God's presence each day as individuals and each week as communities of faith. If we "seek the welfare of our city," we will flourish as it flourishes for all the people.

My sincere hope and prayer is that people from all corners

of society will say "YES" to gratitude as God's kingdom breaks out all around us. At the center of a grateful heart is humble service to others in creative, innovative ways.

Will you hoist your sails to the winds of God's spirit? If you will, then I truly believe you will discover the joy of a grateful heart, a heart of service and love for all people in God's good world.

Reflection and Action

1. Conduct a "heart check" honestly, considering whether you have a grateful heart.

2. In what ways does gathering together as the "people of God" help you become more grateful?

3. What dream do you have for transforming some part of your community to improve people's lives?

4. How can you begin a process of making that dream into a reality of God's kingdom coming on earth?

CHAPTER SIX

Generosity and a Holy Discontent

I rejoice in the Lord greatly that now at last you have revived your concern for me; indeed, you were concerned for me but had no opportunity to show it. Not that I am referring to being in need, for I have learned to be content with whatever I have. I know what it is to have little, and I know what it is to have plenty. In any and all circumstances I have learned the secret of being well-fed and of going hungry, of having plenty and of being in need. I can do all things through him who strengthens me. In any case, it was kind of you to share my distress.

You Philippians indeed know that in the early days of the gospel, when I left Macedonia, no church shared with me in the matter of giving and receiving except you alone. For even when I was in Thessalonica, you sent me help for my needs more than once. Not that I seek the gift, but I seek the profit that accumulates to your account. I have been paid in full and have more than enough; I am fully satisfied, now that I have received from Epaphroditus the gifts you sent, a fragrant offering, a sacrifice acceptable and pleasing to God. And my God will fully satisfy every need of yours according to his riches in glory in Christ Jesus. To our God and Father be glory forever and ever. Amen.

Philippians 4:10-20 (NRSV)

So far, I have mainly discussed the meaning of gratitude from a biblical perspective, which is primarily a matter of what happens within you personally. But now it is time to begin our pivot toward a gratitude that is ultimately expressed in a generosity that arises out of what I call a "holy discontent."

Holy discontent is the sort of restlessness that we can find all the way back to the time of Abraham, who followed the call of God, although he did not know where he was going:

> *Now the Lord said to Abram, "Go from your country and your kindred and your father's house to the land that I will show you. I will make of you a great nation, and I will bless you and make your name great, so that you will be a blessing. I will bless those who bless you, and the one who curses you I will curse, and in you all the families of the earth shall be blessed."*
>
> *So Abram went, as the Lord had told him, and Lot went with him. Abram was seventy-five years old when he departed from Haran. Abram took his wife Sarai and his brother's son Lot and all the possessions that they had gathered and the persons whom they had acquired in Haran, and they set forth to go to the land of Canaan. When they had come to the land of Canaan, Abram passed through the land to the place at Shechem, to the oak of Moreh. At that time the Canaanites were in the land. Then the Lord appeared to Abram and said, "To your offspring I will give this land." So he built there an altar to the Lord, who had appeared to him. From there he moved on to the hill country on the east of Bethel and pitched his tent, with Bethel on the west and Ai on the east, and there he built an altar to the Lord and invoked the name of the Lord. And Abram journeyed on by stages toward the Negeb.*
>
> **Genesis 12:1–9 (NRSV)**

The writer of Hebrews alluded to this concept of a "holy discontentment":

> *By faith Abraham obeyed when he was called to set out for a place that he was to receive as an inheritance, and he set out, not knowing where he was going. By faith he stayed for a time in the land he had been promised, as in a foreign land, living in tents, as did Isaac and Jacob, who were heirs with him of the same promise. For he looked forward to the city that has foundations, whose architect and builder is God. By faith, with Sarah's involvement,*

he received power of procreation, even though he was too old, because he considered him faithful who had promised. Therefore from one person, and this one as good as dead, descendants were born, "as many as the stars of heaven and as the innumerable grains of sand by the seashore."

All of these died in faith without having received the promises, but from a distance they saw and greeted them. They confessed that they were strangers and foreigners on the earth, for people who speak in this way make it clear that they are seeking a homeland. If they had been thinking of the land that they had left behind, they would have had opportunity to return. But as it is, they desire a better homeland, that is, a heavenly one. Therefore, God is not ashamed to be called their God; indeed, he has prepared a city for them.

Hebrews 11:8-16 (NRSVue)

A holy discontent prevents us from focusing only on a personal pursuit for that elusive "Goldilocks moment" in time—a feeling that we have finally arrived at some state of personal contentment where we can enjoy focusing only on ourselves. This misunderstanding of *contentment* sanctions a disregard for our neighbors in our own communities. But scripture calls us to a better way—a holy discontent with the way things are, like having a rock in your shoe.

We can clearly see systemic injustice on state, national, and global levels. We must do the necessary God-inhabited work of shining a very bright light into those dark places. But it must first begin in our own hearts, lives, backyards, and communities in which we live, work, attend church, and send our kids to school. It is not an "either/or" question. It is "both/and." Gratitude also calls us to a deeper way of living that ultimately leads not just to our own transformation but to the transformation of our world.

Many years ago, when I began seminary, I discovered a field of study called "practical theology." Now, to me, that sounded like an oxymoron—you know, like jumbo shrimp, small crowd, instant classic, found missing, or pretty ugly. The phrase "practical theology" seemed to imply that there is also impractical theology. So, as a young seminary student, I wondered, "What's the point of theology if there's no practical application?"

Well, after several years of theological education, I realized that I could spend an entire lifetime contemplating the mysteries of God and God's revelation to us. I could spend all my days trying to understand the conundrums of the Bible and the problem of evil. I could do endless dissertations on the nature of the Trinity and the doctrine of the Atonement.

But at some point along the theological track, you must jump off the theoretical train and enter into the mess of humanity. This is where we begin to pivot from *theory about God* to the practice of *participating with God* in the world. Hence, the field of study is called "practical theology." (And in true contradictory fashion, much of practical theology—i.e., how we ought to live—is very impractical in the eyes of the world.)

Sometimes being practical and spiritual can feel like trying to pat your head and rub your tummy at the same time. Some Christians seem strong on contemplation but weak on the practical side, while others seem strong on the practical side but weak on the contemplative. But somehow, we need to sync the right spirit with the right practice.

It is not an either/or question. The church and the world need both Marys and Marthas. After all, they are sisters.

Similarly, when it comes to true gratitude and a holy

discontent, we must find a way to do the *right things* for the *right reasons* with the *right spirit.* We need to align our spirit with our actions.

Philippians 4:13 expresses a tremendous spiritual concept: "I can do all things through him who gives me strength" (NIV), a concept that has often been misinterpreted primarily for athletes performing to their maximum potential at modern sporting events. And right after this verse, we read about a practical lesson in giving and receiving—with Paul as the needy recipient and the Philippian church as the generous givers.

Paul's words reveal an important truth for us today: God equips people spiritually as they minister practically, enabling God to achieve God's divine ends through human means of participation. Or to put it more simply, God does extraordinary things through ordinary people when we choose to cooperate with God's spirit at work in the world.

In this Philippians text, *the divine end* was to provide for Paul's needs, and the human means was the people of the Philippian church who gladly participated in that provision. In this text, through the example of the Philippian Christians, we learn what it truly means to be generous followers of Jesus as we continually choose gratitude as our lens for viewing the world.

Even Super Apostle Paul had some anxiety now and then, according to Philippians 4:14. In Paul's case, no church shared in giving to support Paul's missionary activity in the ancient world except for the church at Philippi. The generosity of the Philippian church went way back to Paul's early days of ministry. In Acts 16 and 17, Paul preached the gospel in Philippi, then moved on to Thessalonica and Berea. Paul was a very proud, self-sufficient man—some would say even arrogant. Paul made tents to support himself on his missionary travels so he wouldn't have to be dependent on others. But even Paul needed support from time to time—although like most men, he didn't want to admit it.

Yet in Philippians 4:10-20, we see a glimpse of Paul getting beyond his masculinity for just a moment. We read that the generosity of the Philippian church filled him with gratitude—not only for his sake but for theirs as well. Further, he contends that their gifts are a "fragrant offering, a sacrifice acceptable and pleasing to the nostrils of God." This was a common Old Testament phrase for a burnt offering that smelled sweet in the metaphorical nostrils of God.

Paul is grateful for the physical and financial gifts of the Philippians, but he's also filled with joy for their genuine love and gratitude, which prompted the gift—and that is what is most dear to God.[22]

The Philippian believers got it right. They were doing "practical theology." They had both the *right motivation* and the *right application,* which shows us a great example of being generous Christians. So, I want to take a closer look at how true gratitude leads to true generosity. I believe we can break it down from six different angles.

1. **Being generous begins at a point of need (Phil. 4:14).** The Philippian Christians met Paul at his time of need with true generosity. Paul says that when he was at a point of distress—physically and

---

[22] William Barclay, *The Letter to the Philippians* (Westminster Press, 1975).

perhaps spiritually and emotionally—that is when the generosity of the Philippians met him. This true generosity begins when we open our eyes and ears to the needs around us. And often, it involves sharing where there is little or no possibility of reciprocity. So, first, being a generous Christian requires loving, caring, sacrificial action—such as in the story of the Good Samaritan. Loving God AND neighbor are nonnegotiables of the Good News!

2. **True generosity is based upon a spiritual principle (Phil. 4:15).** It's important to understand principles because principles always underlie a truth. For instance, if your car won't start, then you're experiencing the result of a principle. The problem may have to do with the principle of combustion, the principle of ignition, or some other principle, but you can be sure that there's an underlying principle at the root of the problem. This can also happen physically, emotionally, or spiritually when we choose to ignore the underlying principles, and eventually, we suffer the consequences.

   Some Christians never stop to think about how things work spiritually until there's an absolute breakdown. Well, the underlying principle of generosity is found in the phrase "giving and receiving." Jesus said in Matthew 10:8: "You received without payment; give without payment" (NRSV); or "Freely you have received; freely give" (NIV); or "You have been treated generously, so live generously" (MSG). So, sharing with others is a loving response rooted in the generosity and goodness of God. True generosity is not prompted by pity or pressure or personal recognition but by the grace of God. We love, we care, we give—because he first loved us.

3. **True generosity is persistent (Phil. 4:16).** The Philippians gave again and again and again. Paul spoke of their generosity and referred to them as examples. They gave out of their poverty—not their abundance—and were always ready for opportunities to give even more. So, we need to understand that true generosity is not a "one and done" kind of thing. It's not giving because you've got leftover time or money this year. True generosity can't be confined to a designated day on the calendar or a seasonal offering. We share daily, give daily, love daily, and care daily—over and over and over again.

4. **True generosity does not expect payback (Phil. 4:17).** In the previous verses, Paul made it clear that he had learned how to be content in all circumstances. He wasn't seeking a gift for himself; his greater interest was the fruit of true generosity in their lives. And please don't get the false impression that this is primarily about what you give financially to your local church or nonprofit. This is about a disposition toward God and our fellow human beings. This is about saying a kind word, showing compassion, doing social justice, using the gifts that God has given to you, AND giving out of what we have been given. Being rewarded is not why we are generous Christians, and it seldom comes on this earth anyway. But Jesus did say, "Whoever gives a cup of cold water … will certainly not lose his reward" (Matt. 10:42). When it comes to true generosity, the only way to lose is to fail to share.

5. **True generosity brings pleasure (Phil. 4:18).** The pleasure of sharing is a two-way street. Paul was pleased to receive the generous gift, and I'm sure the Philippians were pleased when they heard how Paul described their giving to others. But most importantly, God was pleased by their generosity. Just as children

bring deep pleasure to their parents when they treat each other with kindness, we bring God pleasure as God's children when God sees us becoming more generous like his own son in our actions.

6. **True generosity trusts in God's provision (Phil. 4:19).** God doesn't want the generous person to suffer because of their generosity. God promises to supply all our needs "according to his riches in glory in Christ Jesus." But notice that God doesn't promise to solve all our problems. God supplies according to his riches. In other words, God always supplies in a way that is consistent with God's character. Don't expect to win the lottery because you did God a favor by writing a check to the church. Don't expect to be recognized as "volunteer of the year" just because you brought canned food items for the food pantry. The American "prosperity gospel" has done so much damage in discrediting the church and bringing blatant false teachings into people's living rooms. Further, the gospel that is often being peddled today by politicians and Christian nationalist preachers bears absolutely no resemblance to the one who proclaimed:

    > *Therefore I tell you, do not worry about your life, what you will eat or what you will drink, or about your body, what you will wear. Is not life more than food and the body more than clothing? Look at the birds of the air: they neither sow nor reap nor gather into barns, and yet your heavenly Father feeds them. Are you not of more value than they? And which of you by worrying can add a single hour to your span of life? And why do you worry about clothing? Consider the lilies of the field, how they grow; they neither toil nor spin, yet I tell you, even Solomon in all his glory was not clothed like one of these. But if God so clothes the grass of the field, which is alive today and tomorrow is thrown into the oven, will he not much more clothe you—you of*

little faith? Therefore do not worry, saying, "What will we eat?" or "What will we drink?" or "What will we wear?" For it is the gentiles who seek all these things, and indeed your heavenly Father knows that you need all these things. But seek first the kingdom of God and his righteousness, and all these things will be given to you as well.

So do not worry about tomorrow, for tomorrow will bring worries of its own. Today's trouble is enough for today.

Matthew 6:25-34 (NRSVue)

Contentment is an elusive state of being in our modern world. And it is peddled as a normative self-focused attempt to be "happy." We are called to be "content in Christ" but to also have a "holy discontent" with the way things are when people are excluded, marginalized, and treated unfairly.

What God promises to us is his provision for all our needs as we practice true generosity, trust, and gratitude. Being contented, grateful Christians has to do with how we practice our speech, how we treat others, and how we give from what God has blessed us with. We need a major course correction today about how Jesus actually portrays his Heavenly Father in the Gospels: loving, compassionate, and just. Maybe it's time to overturn some tables.

There is an old tale that goes something like this:

One evening, an old chief told his grandson about a battle that goes on inside people.

He said, "My son, the battle is between two wolves. One is Evil. It is anger, envy, sorrow, regret, greed, arrogance, self-pity, guilt, resentment, inferiority, lies, false pride, superiority, and ego."

> *"The other is Good. It is joy, peace, love, hope, serenity, humility, kindness, benevolence, empathy, generosity, truth, compassion, and faith."*
>
> *The grandson thought about it for a minute and then asked, "Grandfather, which wolf wins?"*
>
> *The old chief simply replied, "The one you feed always wins."*

It is in our words, actions, attitudes, and giving that we see true generosity expressed—or not. We fight a constant battle between the two wolves. Which one we feed determines how we experience life and how we affect the lives of those around us.

So, don't waste your time with a distortion of the gospel that is primarily "all about me." And please don't display a false generosity by giving under reluctance, compulsion, or pressure—whether it's your time, money, or compassion. God only wants cheerful, hilarious givers whose only return is the deep joy and satisfaction they receive by practicing true generosity to all people—especially "the least of these"—from a heart of gratitude.

Paul sums up true generosity:

> *The point is this: the one who sows sparingly will also reap sparingly, and the one who sows generously will also reap generously.*
>
> *Each of you must give as you have made up your mind, not reluctantly or under compulsion, for God loves a cheerful giver.*
>
> **2 Corinthians 9:6-7 (NRSV)**

Reflection and Action

1. After reading these words of Paul, we can feel the pathos of just how moved Paul was by the generosity of God and God's people. The only words he had left were a fitting note of praise and worship: "And my God will fully satisfy every need of yours according to his riches in glory in Christ Jesus. To our God and Father be glory forever and ever. Amen" (Phil. 4:19-20, NRSV). Have you ever had a similar experience of receiving an unexpected gift of generosity from someone? If so, how did that experience make you feel?

2. When was the last time you remember having the feeling of genuine contentment? What were your circumstances at that time? And how did those circumstances contribute to, or take away from, your contentment?

3. Please share with your group, or write down, what the following verses found in Philippians 4:12-13 mean to you:
   - "I know what it is to have little, and I know what it is to have plenty."
   - "In any and all circumstances, I have learned the secret of being well-fed and of going hungry, of having plenty and of being in need."
   - "I can do all things through him who strengthens me."

4. How can a follower of Jesus possess "contentment" and a "holy discontent" with the way things are in the world at the same time?

5. In what new ways can you envision moving forward with genuine gratitude to participate in "the kingdom of God coming on earth as it is in heaven?"

And now we are ready to move into the second half of this book ...

Part Two:

Gratitude From Us to Our Communities

First Baptist Church – Mount Olive, North Carolina

CHAPTER SEVEN

One Congregation's Story

On November 18, 2021, as I concluded a sermon series on gratitude, I issued a challenge from the pulpit to the good people of First Baptist Church in Mount Olive, North Carolina, that, as a congregation, we should set aside $100,000 as an expression of our gratitude to God and invest these funds in the neediest parts of our community. I explained that we could do that by awarding grants to local nonprofits and individuals who share a passion for closing the "gratitude gap," as asserted by Diana Butler-Bass:

> *There is a gratitude gap between what we believe and what we practice ... that we may be thankful in private, but individual gratitude doesn't appear to make much difference in our larger common life together.*[23]

If I am honest, I was a bit nervous because I was not sure how this proposal would go over. After all, we were still reeling from the great uncertainty of the COVID-19 pandemic, shrinking attendance, and a tight economy. We also happened to live in a community with one of the highest poverty rates in North Carolina.

But I felt strongly that this was exactly what God wanted me to put forth, so I did. I made this ambitious proposal without talking to any committees, deacons, councils, or trustees beforehand.

---

[23] Diane Butler Bass, *Grateful.*

Now, this was not my customary practice, and I am not recommending that you follow my example. My leadership style has always been about building consensus before making church-wide proposals. But this was different. I was out on a limb all by myself. Courageous or crazy. It could have gone either way.

As I planned a series of sermons on gratitude for my own church in 2021, I honestly had no idea that I would conclude it the way I did. But this was where God's Spirit led me—and I do believe in hoisting my sails to the winds of the Spirit, not knowing ahead of time just where God might lead.

God had blessed our church financially in an amazing way over the past twenty years, placing good and wise people to manage and oversee its resources and assets. And for these folks, we were deeply grateful. However, I told the congregation that I believed the time had come for us to give back freely and joyfully out of our abundance.

Our mission statement proclaimed, "We seek to be the presence of Christ in the world by fulfilling the great commandment and great commission," which tells us to love God with all that we are and to love our neighbors as ourselves as we go into all the world discipling and baptizing people from all nations.

So, I said, "What would it look like to make our mission statement a reality in our community? In what ways might it look differently from today? It's time to close the 'gratitude gap' by targeting the greatest human needs around us with a greater portion of the resources that God has sent our way—to become the presence of Christ to our community."

Yes, we accomplished some amazing things over the years to touch our community, such as:

- COATS for KIDS and Warm the World
- Partnering with Habitat for Humanity to build over ten new homes in Mount Olive
- Partnering with Haitian and Hispanic congregations and reaching out to immigrants
- Partnering with our local schools, providing bikes for children and international college students
- Distributing thousands of dollars every year to assist residents with their power and water bills

But on that day, I was proposing that we take it to the next level. After twenty years of being their pastor, if I couldn't pull this off, then it might be time to pack it in. After all the upheaval from COVID and the divisive cultural shifts of the past decade, I was not interested in pouring my efforts into "making the church great again" by finding magical ways to bring back the past—reaching all those mythical young families that once upon a time filled the pews of our sanctuary.

In our small eastern North Carolina town, the reality is that there are only a limited number of young, middle-class families with children. Most of those who grow up here go off to college and never move back. Of course, I still wanted to reach young families, but in the last decade of my ministry, my passion had become more focused on helping bring "the kingdom of God in my community just as it is in heaven," which meant getting directly involved in impacting the poorest residents of our community simply out of gratitude for God's love and grace.

It was time for us to do more to reach out to our church's neighbors, most of whom are on the lower end of the socioeconomic ladder. To be clear, this was not going to be a "bait and switch" program. I was not proposing that the ultimate goal be getting more "butts in the pews." This new venture had to be about giving joyfully, purely, and out of the resources God had blessed us with—no strings attached.

God had blessed our congregation in many ways—especially with a large estate gift from a faithful church member in 2003, which our trustees had stewarded wisely over the years. In addition, the church owned two tracts of land that were leased for solar farming alongside traditional agricultural farming. Because of these assets, we had accumulated some financial reserves that I believed could be invested as an expression of gratitude to benefit the people of our community who needed it most.

So, after several informational meetings with the congregation, in February 2022, the congregation gave unanimous approval to the birth of "The Gratitude Project," which would result in $100,000 being invested in community development for our small town—targeting poverty, affordable housing, educational opportunities for children and youth, and economic progress among the poor.

This project would focus on holistically transforming lives in our community, primarily through local organizations and nonprofits that share our common mission. We did not need to duplicate the good work already being done. We simply needed to let go of some assets to empower those groups to do even more.

So, off we went on an uncharted journey with no prior experience in community development. This project was about transforming lives and bringing God's kingdom on earth—not about growing a church of homogeneous people who look and think alike. And I am deeply grateful that the congregation trusted me and said "yes" to a fresh new approach of "being the presence of Christ" in our community.

The Gratitude Project helped our congregation reframe our mission. It all begins with gratitude of the heart—sincere gratitude; gratitude that is neither coerced nor programmed; gratitude that is good news for the poor, release for the captives, and a gift available to all neighbors for such a time as this.

This mission may or may not result in traditional church growth. It will most definitely involve learning and making mistakes. Ultimately, the church of the 21st century desperately needs many fresh approaches to move us toward our mission of "being the presence of Christ in the world" and transforming lives with the good news of Christ.

However, transformative gratitude must be cultivated, taught, and modeled with intent. It involves the painful process of letting go of attitudes and assets that we hold onto with a mighty death grip, constantly encouraged by our self-focused, scarcity-minded culture.

This is our current reality, and it must be intentionally reversed if congregations are to become thriving, diverse communities of faith. Gratitude is at the very heart of this resurrection enterprise of new life.

Jeremiah 29:7 says, "Seek the welfare of the city where I have sent you … and pray to the Lord on its behalf, for in its welfare you will find your welfare" (NRSVue). This was one of the verses that helped shape the details of The Gratitude Project: "to seek the welfare of the city."

The idea was that, for one to two years, a process would be established to allow individuals and groups within our congregation and community to apply for grants. These grants would fund innovative projects specifically aimed at alleviating poverty, substandard housing, and unemployment, as well as strengthening education and the quality of life for children and families in the Mount Olive community.

This money would not be benevolence funds. Instead, this project would focus on investing in sustainable ways in the neediest areas—efforts that support our church's mission and help our community flourish.

Just imagine the impact that could be made in one year by spreading $100,000 across a dozen projects throughout our community—planting seeds of gratitude and hope—trusting God with the results. And it would transform our own discipleship.

The question then was, "What are we waiting for?"

Every congregation has resources—if we will use them. And there will never be a better time than the present to give back to your community where it is needed most.

OUR MODEL

In his book *Toxic Charity,* Robert Lupton writes, "Contrary to popular belief, most mission trips and service projects do not:

- Empower those being served
- Engender healthy cross-cultural relationships
- Improve local quality of life
- Relieve poverty
- Change the lives of participants
- Increase support for long-term mission work

Contrary to popular belief, most mission trips and service projects do:

- Weaken those being served
- Foster dishonest relationships
- Erode the recipient's work ethic
- Deepen dependency[24]

Having spent two summers in Africa and having taken college students and church members on dozens of mission trips and local service projects, I would generally agree with Lupton's assessment—although I have witnessed exceptions.

I had no desire to contribute to the old mission model of doing for others, which primarily makes volunteers feel good without actually bringing about lasting transformation in the lives of people and systems in the local community. I wanted The Gratitude Project to be different—a fresh model that empowers those already doing great work in the community to do even more, while also tapping into the innovative ideas of laity who have a passion for service but lack a runway in the church to help launch their visions into reality.

---

[24] Robert Lupton, *Toxic Charity* (New York: HarperCollins, 2011).

This is research and development (R&D) for the 21st-century church. Through many attempts and failures, led by the Spirit, we will find ways to connect assets with needs that ultimately contribute to sustainable change and transformation in us and our communities. And here's the kicker—it starts with a genuine spirit of gratitude alongside those whom we seek to help.

I hope that this book will be a primer for you and your people—congregation or friend group—to go "stir up some good trouble" by letting go of outdated methods, structures, and ineffective models of service and create fresh, innovative ways of further revealing God's kingdom at hand in our local communities.

It's time to let go of old attitudes, dead programs, and God-given assets for the benefit of the people who live in the communities where our church buildings are located. And we must also learn creative ways to open our church buildings and spaces for community use and nontraditional ministries.

As word got out about The Gratitude Project, I received a call from the Food Bank of Central and Eastern North Carolina about First Baptist of Mount Olive hosting a "pop-up food market" in our parking lot once a month. And of course, I said, "Yes, please."

In our first year (2023), we served over 5,000 individuals and 1,741 households; distributed 88,336 pounds of food and 76,613 meals! Feeding over 5,000 people fresh food and produce during our very first year left quite an impact on our community for a small church.

Another ripple effect came from a totally different direction. The Wayne County Arts Council had recently lost its lease, and we had an abundance of unused space in our large education building. Again, word had gotten out about our willingness to innovate space for the benefit of the community.

After several meetings with the Arts Council board members, the church invited the organization to utilize our seldom-used second-floor space to set up art and music studios for local artists. This initiative marked the beginning of a unique partnership that brought the arts into the church. The Gratitude Project kicked in $10,000 for future scholarships to economically disadvantaged children and youth who wish to receive art or music lessons from the Arts Council.

Community transformation cooks more like a crockpot than a microwave. It doesn't cook quickly. But when we begin with a heart of gratitude in a posture of possibilities, there is no limit to the transformation God's Spirit can bring!

I am confident that these "ripple effects" will continue—as long as we let go of our self-centered attitudes and build assets in a spirit of gratitude for the benefit of our community. The possibilities for participating in the transformation of our communities are endless.

In the next section, I will provide a model for starting something comparable to The Gratitude Project. I simply offer this as one example that can be adapted to the context of your communities. Consider it "R&D" for your group or congregation.

First Steps

In our case, after appointing a four-person committee to oversee The Gratitude Project, we began taking our first steps, including developing a solid theological and practical foundation to move this idea from theory to practice. So, first, we developed an application, guidelines, and a website.

Here is a description of our initial plan.

What?

The congregation of First Baptist Church of Mount Olive set aside $100,000 to be invested in "community development" in our local area. These funds are specifically aimed at alleviating poverty, improving affordable housing, strengthening economic opportunities for children and youth, and encouraging economic growth in Mount Olive.

The project encourages a diversity of impact areas within its overall goal. Recipients will receive project-specific operating funding over the course of one year.

Why?

According to the U.S. Census Bureau in 2020, among residents of the Town of Mount Olive, 60 percent of those living in poverty are either under eighteen or sixty-five or older.

The Gratitude Project is a gift to our community, a token of our gratitude for God's abundant blessings over the years. It is also another step toward fulfilling the Great Commandment to "love our neighbor as ourselves" in line with our mission statement of "being the presence of Christ in the world."

How?

The process for funding innovative projects and ministries is based upon the awarding of grants by a fund committee to individual members of First Baptist Church of Mount Olive who are encouraged to match their spiritual gifts and passions with "needs and poverty points" in the community.

In addition, local grassroots community organizations and nonprofits may apply for grant funds with proposals consistent with the church's mission and The Gratitude Project's purpose.

Applications are submitted to The Gratitude Project fund committee through a clearly defined process, along with a detailed ministry/action plan to make a lasting impact among the poorest within our community. Once a grant proposal is approved, the individual or group must agree to report back to the congregation on the impact and outcomes of their project during our Sunday morning worship service within six to twelve months.

Guiding Principles for the Gratitude Project

1. Invest in people to live out their faith at work.
2. Address poverty and other social challenges in Mount Olive.
3. Provide a way for members of First Baptist to connect with and support the initiative.
4. Include a sustainable plan to live beyond the initial investment from The Gratitude Project.
5. Invest in opportunities that:
    - Contribute to the spiritual formation process for recipients to live out their faith in the world.
    - Leverage our members' strengths, passions, and experience to positively impact the poorest areas of Mount Olive.

- Demonstrate potential for long-term social impact on the town of Mount Olive.
- Accelerate or launch lasting, sustainable programs.

6. All applicants must complete the initial online application. Applications require the following information and documentation:
   - Contact information, including name, address, phone number, and email address.
   - A brief description of the project in one sentence.
   - A more detailed, one-paragraph executive summary that answers the following four questions:
     i. What is the problem you are trying to solve?
     ii. How will you solve it?
     iii. What are your intended outcomes (how will your solution address the lives you wish to serve)?
     iv. How does your faith inform your idea?
7. Initial applications through the screening process are reviewed and evaluated on the following: feasibility, problem understanding, innovation, and congruence with the mission of First Baptist Church.

During our first year of implementation, we were shocked at just how few serious applications we received. I saw early on that it can be quite complicated to award money to worthwhile projects when you require a coherent, sustainable proposal that holds the recipient accountable for their spending and outcomes. But doing it the right way requires patience and resilience.

Eventually, we began accumulating applications that we sifted through prayerfully, staying true to our original mission and purpose. In the next chapter, I will offer a brief description of several grants that were awarded during The Gratitude Project.

Reflection and Action

1. What parts of The Gratitude Project model could you imagine working in your own community, if any? Why or why not?

2. What are the greatest needs in your community among the poorest residents? Make a list.

3. What are your individual, group, and congregation's greatest assets? Make a list for all three.

4. Now, brainstorm about how God might use your individual and collective assets to creatively connect with the specific needs of specific people in your immediate community. Write down everyone's thoughts and then step back and take a look.

5. Why do you think it is so important to do this exercise with a "posture of possibilities"?

6. Are you honestly open and ready to meet the needs of your community with your time and resources? Is your group, or congregation?

CHAPTER EIGHT

The Gratitude Project and Lessons Learned

For this book, I will not go into detail about each grant recipient, but I want to mention a few. The primary reason is that I hope to inspire you to dream your own original dreams about what might work in your community when you connect your assets and gifts with the needs—physical, spiritual, educational, emotional, financial, and spiritual—that exist right where you live and worship.

The Gratitude Project was a good fit for our congregation and community—time and place. The Gratitude Project model might work for you, and it might not.

The real question is this: Given my/our gifts, resources, and abilities, and considering the greatest needs that are currently NOT being addressed among the underserved in our community, how might God be calling me/us to bridge those gaps?

There are indeed "gratitude gaps," as Diana Butler Bass asserts, because we would already be erasing those gaps if we were properly filled with biblical gratitude.

The very first application came from one of our own members, Janet Rose, who also played the piano for our worship. She called her initiative "Keys to Success." The Holy Spirit had stirred this idea within her heart when she first heard the concept of The Gratitude Project.

In her own words, "Keys to Success is my idea to provide a means for musically talented, underprivileged children to receive piano lessons and a piano for practicing in their home. My goal is to increase the number of trained musicians available in the community and churches." Her hope was to ensure that children interested in learning piano had access to lessons, the necessary materials, and a piano at home—giving them the chance to develop music as a lifelong skill.

Another funded project went to a local nonprofit, All the King's Children, for an after-school learning lab consisting of educational, hands-on programs that provide children with the skills needed and the opportunity to become independent, productive members of the community.

One nontraditional grant went to a local football program under the leadership of the Fellowship of Christian Athletes. The program served a high percentage of underprivileged children from predominantly single-parent households, who were mentored and coached by Christian men—men committed to coaching them "beyond the game." Their glaring need was for new, safer equipment. Without new helmets and pads, the football program would have been discontinued.

One of our town's biggest needs is affordable housing. Enter into the picture WARM NC (Wilmington Area Remodeling Ministry). Their initiative, "Hope for Housing," offers free home repairs to low-income homeowners. In doing so, WARM NC creates safer homes, provides a wealth-building opportunity for families, and helps retain affordable housing for the community.

As an example of how each person and group plays a vital role in community improvement, CEO Andy Jones stated:

This truly was a community effort. A social worker referred "Mr. Robert," who was disabled, to us. Pastor Atwood helped our client get all his necessary paperwork together for approval. The Gratitude Project provided $18,000 in funding, which, with matching grants provided through WARM NC, became $73,000 in funding for repairs. WARM NC provided the contractors and First United Methodist Church of Morganton, North Carolina, provided the volunteers.

During The Gratitude Project, the Arts Council of Wayne County, North Carolina, entered into a partnership with First Baptist Mount Olive to lease space in the church to house studios for local and area artists. As part of our agreement, the Arts Council was asked to conduct an annual children's camp at the church facilities, while The Gratitude Project provided scholarships for campers in need of financial assistance.

In addition to the groups mentioned above, by the end of 2024, The Gratitude Project had also awarded grants to nonprofits such as the local Wayne County Library for summer reading programs, our local public Carver Elementary School for outdoor basketball goals, and WAGES Community Action, designated for affordable housing opportunities in Mount Olive. So, by the end of the project, a total of $100,000 was strategically invested in our community. Yes, it was a drop in the bucket, but one that will be creating ripples for many years to come.

Ten Lessons Learned from Launching this Project

There's an old saying that goes: If you aim at nothing, you'll hit it every time. This is actually an exciting time to be a Christ-follower who is willing to be adventurous and innovative in their faith and mission, with a posture of possibilities.

It is important to understand that this kind of faith must be willing to fail, to learn from those failed experiments, and to adapt accordingly. The safe bet is to aim at nothing or keep doing what you've always done. But that simply won't cut it in a post-Christian, post-pandemic world.

So, if you choose to be innovative in your mission, get ready to make some mistakes, ruffle some feathers, and stir up some "good trouble." You will learn what most needs to be done, what things can be left behind, and the messiness of doing missions in your own community. This includes the surprising reality that helping people can be really complicated.

Here are ten lessons we learned in launching an innovative approach to impact our community through The Gratitude Project:

1. **Do a "heart check.** Before launching into a new innovative initiative, make sure you have laid enough groundwork. In other words, take the pulse of your people. Preparing their hearts may take weeks, months, or even years. In my case, I had spent twenty years doing the work of a pastor before I threw something like this at them. The first six chapters of this book offer a taste of what biblical gratitude means and how to cultivate it. We must allow God to transform our own hearts and minds before we can bring lasting transformation to our communities.

2. **Hoist Your Sails to the Winds of God's Spirit**. In her book *Sailboat Church: Helping Your Church Rethink Its Mission and Practice,* author Joan Gray sums this up perfectly:

> *The attitude in the rowboat congregation is either "WE can do this," or "WE can't do this" ... focusing on circumstances ... and our own strength, wisdom, and resources. It's all about how hard, long, and well people are willing to row ... Rowboat churches tend toward a mindset of scarcity ... If we believe that God has left us alone to do the work of the church by ourselves, we will row.*[25]

In contrast, "sailboat churches" focus on the power of the Spirit at work within us to do far more than we can ask or imagine. They focus not on their own situation, resources, or limitations, but rather on discerning the unfolding will of God. They "know that they cannot make the wind blow, but they realize they can tap into spiritual resources beyond themselves by reorienting their efforts and catching the wind of God's Spirit!"[26]

3. **Be Transparent.** Let all your work and planning be available for anyone in your congregation to see. Bless those who curse you or your project—and there will probably be a few.

4. **Be Accountable.** Whether you primarily focus on nonprofits or individuals, focus on those who already have a stellar reputation in your community for integrity and for being effective at what they do.

5. **Communicate regularly with fund recipients and the congregation.** This strengthens the relationship between the congregation and the community. Sometimes, despite our good intentions and pure hearts, false information spreads. Communicate, communicate, and communicate some more.

---

[25] Joan Gray, *Sailboat Church: Helping Your Church Rethink Its Mission and Practice* (Westminster John Knox Press, 2014).

[26] Joan Gray, *Sailboat Church.*

6. **Be persistent.** It takes hard work, clarity of purpose, and resilience to help the people who need it most. If (when) you make mistakes, learn from them and keep moving forward toward your goal and purpose.

7. **Expect the unexpected.** Once tossed into a sea of human needs, there will be ripple effects coming your way that you never dreamed of—mostly positive ripples. This is what I referred to earlier as a "posture of possibilities," meaning that we pay attention, we look and listen for the hopeful signs of God's presence and guidance—every day.

8. **Be ready for some waves of negativity.** Not everyone in your community wants to see you succeed. Think slumlords or those profiting off the backs of the poor. But the call for justice and mercy cannot be left to others.

9. **Be prepared for outright opposition.** I was not. When I tried to convene a "Summit on Affordable Housing" in my community, I was slandered, and fliers were put out all around town falsely claiming that I was "bringing in illegal immigrants who will move into your neighborhoods, bring down your property values, destroy your educational system, and make your community filled with crime." So, the reality in these volatile, politically charged times is that following the Jesus of the New Testament will get you in trouble, or politicized, or even worse, get you accused of being "woke."

10. **Plan diligently, but be prepared to adapt your plans as you go.** See numbers 8 and 9, but please do this work with joy and gratitude—at all times, if possible. Always keep your purpose before you and stand in solidarity with the poor among us.

Reflection and Action

1. In what ways can you challenge your friends and congregation to dream up your own version of The Gratitude Project?

2. Have you ever been passionate about an idea for meeting real human needs in your community, only to have it shut down or wilt away for lack of support or energy?

3. If so, how did that make you feel then, and what is stopping you from pushing forward right now?

Dennis Atwood, 2021

CHAPTER NINE

Lessons I Am Learning in My Journey with Parkinson's

We have covered the story of one ordinary congregation that chose to do something innovative for their community out of gratitude for the goodness of God and God's blessings upon their life together as a community of faith. Now it is time to circle back to your own personal journey. This is a "rinse and repeat" kind of journey we are all on. It is NOT: "I have learned, therefore, I have finally arrived as an expert."

So, it's time to get honest with God, with yourself, and maybe with each other about the possibilities of gratitude transforming us and our communities. I will go first.

As I circle back to my own journey, I realize just how much Parkinson's has affected my life and family. If Parkinson's disease does nothing else, it constantly humbles you … every single day … relentlessly. Anyone who has a chronic illness, a family member or close friend going through a "dark night of the soul," as St. John of the Cross put it, understands this. It is amazing how often learning to live with a chronic illness (Parkinson's in my case) intersects with learning how to navigate the road of discipleship as a Christ-follower—while carrying a genuine spirit of gratitude.

So, I want to take a moment to describe ten lessons I am learning—or relearning—as I live with Parkinson's disease as a person of faith. I hope some of these will resonate with your story as well.

1. **I am learning that perfectionism and Parkinson's cannot co-exist.** This is a tough one for me. For as long as I can remember, I have possessed an innate drive to do everything as perfectly as possible. In sports, relationships, and work, I needed to be the absolute best version of myself—all the time. Maybe it has something to do with being a middle child. I don't really know. It is just in my nature. Believe me, I did not ask for this! As you might guess, this tendency does not mix well with a neurological disorder that progressively takes away your ability to strive toward perfection. Not to mention there's that line in the Sermon on the Mount where Jesus says, Oh, and by the way, you should also be perfect, just as your Heavenly Father is perfect. This is where paying attention in Greek class actually transformed my thinking about perfectionism.

   The New Testament Greek word most commonly translated as "perfect" in the Bible is teleios (τέλειος), meaning wholeness, completeness, maturity, and fulfilling a purpose, as in striving for God's character in the verse: "Be perfect, as your Heavenly Father is perfect" (Matthew 5:48, NIV). There is no higher aspiration one can have. So, I think I can strive towards that—strive for God and God's kingdom. At the same time, I understand that I will never accomplish this to "perfection." Striving to grow into the character, or qualities, of our Heavenly Father is what the Beatitudes is all about—acknowledging our own poverty of spirit with an utter dependence on our Creator, mourning with those who are suffering, exhibiting meekness and humility, having a passion for righteousness and justice, showing mercy to everyone, living with an undivided devotion to God Almighty, working actively for peace, being willing to suffer for what is right. This is what our Father in heaven looks like. So, I don't have to be perfect—and you don't either. We just need to have a little more grace for ourselves, as we strive first and foremost for God and God's kingdom above all else.

2. **I am learning that humility is an absolute requirement.** Just the other day, I spent three hours in the walk-in clinic at my local doctor's office. The day before, I was looking for my water bottle around the house. I took a few steps into the bathroom and didn't see it. As I was backing out of the doorway, the next thing I remember was suddenly falling backwards with all my weight crashing down on my tailbone and back. In the Parkinson's world, this is known as "freezing gait." I didn't even have time to move my hands back to break my fall. And this was not a typical fall. No, this was a solid thud. The shooting pain piercing through my lower back was excruciating, and sure enough, I had a mild compression fracture in my back. Just another day in the life with Parkinson's! Whether it's being compelled to retire much earlier than I had planned or dealing with diminished speech and mobility, Parkinson's has a cruel way of slowly but surely chipping away at your pride. Just a smattering of verses from Scripture suggest that God despises pride but looks with compassion and favor upon the humble:

    - *The fear of the Lord is hatred of evil. Pride and arrogance and the way of evil and perverted speech I hate* (Prov. 8:13, NRSVue).

    - *When pride comes, then comes disgrace but wisdom is with the humble* (Prov. 11:2, NRSV).

    - *Blessed are the poor in spirit, for theirs is the kingdom of heaven ... Blessed are the meek, for they will inherit the earth* (Matt. 5:3, 5, NRSV).

    - This one especially hurts ...
      Pride goes before destruction, and a haughty spirit before a fall (Prov. 16:18 NRSV).

3. **I am learning that I must do everything with intent.** See the above as an example. I know that I should not make sudden turns or move my feet backwards, or I will likely lose my balance. What used to come naturally to my brain without giving it a second thought has now become something that I must tell my brain to intentionally practice ... every single time ... every single day. And it can get quite annoying. Sometimes when I don't speak or act with intent, I end up paying the price. The same is true for anyone who wishes to be a follower of Jesus. Loving my neighbor, loving my enemies, denying myself—none of this comes naturally for human beings. No, we must live with intent every single moment and every single day if we are going to seriously take up our cross and follow Jesus.

4. **I am learning how to receive the gracious help of others.** My wife, Ann, is my rock, and she is always telling me, "I will help you if you will just ask." But I don't naturally like to ask for help. I have been in a helping vocation for over thirty years. As a pastor, I have been the one visiting the sick, the bereaved, and the homebound. I have been the one to provide leadership for my family and others. So, it is very difficult for me to turn off that default mode of doing things on my own. Again, life has a way of flipping our roles, plans, and ambitions. But we must still learn to be gracious receivers of help from others—especially from the ones who love us most. I am still trying to figure out how to ask for and accept help from others, and when I don't, I usually pay the price.

5. **I am learning to focus on what I can control rather than what I cannot.** Life with Parkinson's requires constant adjustment and acceptance of new

realities. This includes adapting routines, accepting limitations, and finding new ways to engage with the world. I cannot change the weather. I cannot change my height. I cannot change the past. I cannot change the economy. I cannot change other people. I cannot change the church. I cannot change my Parkinson's diagnosis. And that's just the tip of the iceberg.
But I still have agency. I can choose gratitude or bitterness. I can choose forgiveness or resentment. I can choose peace or chaos. I can choose faith or fear. I can choose hope or despair. I can choose love—which is the greatest of all of these—or I can choose hate. The reality of the human condition is that alone, I can do very little to change most of the circumstances and things life has delivered to me. But there are so many little things I can choose, so that when tossed into the sea of humanity, they send ripples of goodness, kindness, and gratitude across our world, bringing transformation beyond all we can hope for and imagine.

6. **I am learning that my superpower is resiliency.** I have a framed poster that hung in my office for a couple of decades that now resides in my workout room at home. It pictures a lone runner trekking through a vast, barren wilderness, and on the poster, it reads: "DETERMINATION—The race does not always go to the swift, but to those who keep on running." As I think about that picture, it hits me: that has been the subliminal message of my story all along. Whether in sports, education, relationships, or vocation (and now living with Parkinson's), that is what I have done—do the best I can with what I've been given wherever I am. That is all anyone can do, and that will be enough to see you through for today. And today is all we have for certain.

7. **I am learning to find new joy and purpose.** Despite the challenges, it is crucial to find joy and meaning in everyday life. This could involve pursuing hobbies, connecting with loved ones, or engaging in activities that bring a sense of accomplishment. Learning to live in the present moment and appreciate the simple things in life is a valuable lesson from Parkinson's. Even the harshest circumstances we face can be catalysts for reevaluating priorities and finding new meaning and purpose in life.

8. **I am learning the importance of mental, spiritual, and physical health.** Maintaining a healthy lifestyle—including exercise, a balanced diet, and mental and spiritual practices like mindfulness and meditation—is essential for managing symptoms and improving quality of life. I work hard every day at physical exercise, but I know I can only do so much to fight this progressive disease. I have spent a lifetime trying to grow spiritually and challenging others to do the same. But over the years, I have likely neglected my mental health at the expense of caring for others—which is probably common among many pastors. However, we pastors need help too.
   Parkinson's has taken away so much from me over the past two years that I finally admitted I needed to talk with someone. The first counselor I met with said to me, "You know, many Christians believe that God allows sicknesses in order to teach us something. Maybe God wants to teach you something through Parkinson's. I replied, "That is not the God I believe in! What kind of God allows people to get a cruel, degenerative disease like Parkinson's just to teach you a lesson?" As I recall, she replied, "I sense you have anger issues with God." I did not go back to her for any more "counseling" sessions. Eventually, I found a wonderful pastoral counselor who has helped

me work through the grief and loss of things like identity, vocation, and movement that this disease has taken away from me. I am slowly beginning to come to terms with this unwanted intruder called Parkinson's. Everyone needs to have a mental health plan. I have learned that "coming to terms" does not mean giving up. It is more about adapting to this new thing in your life. Do the best you can with what you've been given where you are.

9. **I am learning to seek support, connection, and community.** Connecting with others who understand the challenges of Parkinson's, whether through support groups or online communities, can provide invaluable support and reduce feelings of isolation. Building a strong support network of family, friends, and healthcare professionals is crucial for both the person with Parkinson's and the caregiver. Do not forget the caregiver! They will need time away to recharge their physical, emotional, and spiritual batteries. And let me just insert here that being a pastor can be lonely, but being a "former pastor" is just plain weird. When you serve a church, you have an immediate built-in community. When you are compelled to resign for medical reasons beyond your control, nobody really knows what to say to you or what category to place you in. I can't blame them for that because now, for the first time in my adult life, it's up to me to go out and find my own connection and community. It is a new beginning that takes time to find "your people." But I know I must build a network of relationships for support, connection, and community. It is a basic human need we all share in common, and most of us are still a work in progress. It is a slow process, but a necessary part of becoming good humans.

10. **I am learning to choose gratitude as my default setting for life.** When we choose gratitude—as a daily spiritual practice and as the lens through which we will view God, our neighbors, and our own lives—the possibilities for transformation are endless. Gratitude has the potential to transform all of us and, in turn, the diverse communities in which we live. Our lives and our livelihoods are at stake! God knows in divisive, distorted times like these, a little bit of genuine gratitude goes a long, long way. So, I hope you will join me in accepting the ongoing daily challenge of choosing gratitude. In doing so, we will make this a better world for all of us to live in by choosing gratitude every single day.

Reflection and Action

1. What are you most grateful for in this season of your life?

2. What changes can you make in your life to become a more grateful person?

3. What things hinder you from being more grateful?

4. Make a list of ten lessons you are learning about gratitude.

C.S. Lewis

"God whispers to us in our pleasures, speaks in our conscience, but shouts in our pain: it is His megaphone to rouse a deaf world."

CHAPTER TEN

Writing Your Own Story of Gratitude

So, what's your story? Becoming a participant in the kingdom of God—coming into your community as a foretaste of heaven—is an awesome privilege. We should be filled with gratitude at the opportunity to serve, and it is Jesus-followers who ought to be at the leading edge of transforming our communities for the common good. And again, we do so with gratitude, expecting nothing in return.

Imagine what your community could become if the collective body of Christ in your town or city utilized all its assets to address poverty and food insecurity; improve education, economic development, and job opportunities; strengthen families and neighborhoods; nurture a flourishing spirituality; and stand together in solidarity to demand justice for all people. It might feel like a foretaste of heaven on earth—the kingdom of God here and now.

So, what is preventing you and your group or congregation from pursuing that mission? You cannot do it alone, but someone must get it started. Someone must step up to be the catalyst who launches a fresh, innovative approach for seeking sustainable change by empowering those already engaged in this transformative work to do even more—and not worry about who gets credit.

Consider asking a local social worker or clergy member who specializes in "Asset Mapping" to lead a session in your group for your community. I invited Rev. Dr. Jason Coker, the national director of Together for Hope, to lead such a session for my community, hosted by my church several years ago. It was a fantastic catalyst for launching The Gratitude Project and for learning about the many positive assets that already existed in our church and community—assets we might not have recognized before. It also exposed gaps in services and unmet community needs.

You and your church may not have rainy-day funds or reserves at your disposal, but the scale is less important than the action. You can have a yard sale, sell barbecue plates, host an auction, a car wash, a golf tournament, and more, to raise funds to turn around and award grants to nonprofits, a worthy community service group, or an individual trying to address the concerns of your community. Or you might just dream up something else totally new and outside of the conventional box. Innovation often raises eyebrows and arouses skeptics, but it almost always comes from those who are willing to step up and over the conventional box.

I believe the real work of the kingdom of God is going on outside the sanctuaries that dot our cities and towns, and it is time that we join in that kingdom work—not to get more people in the pews but to simply be better followers of Jesus who choose to do good as an expression of our love and gratitude. Politics, power, and prestige will all fade away. We are citizens of a kingdom not of this world that will never end. So, why don't we act like it?

Kenda Creasy Dean sums up our present situation well:

> *As I see it, the COVID-shaken church has two choices: to patch things up and row back to where we came from, or*

> *to become the church Christ calls us to be, imagining and embodying a new kind of life-giving community to our current situation.*[27]

Did The Gratitude Project transform our entire community? Not hardly, but we did make an impact on people's lives and upon some of the systems in which we are all enmeshed. We were doing our part to "poke holes into the darkness" that surrounds us.

My congregation was small; however, that is not the issue. The issue is whether we will take the resources God has given us and steward them for God's kingdom. We must be faithful to God's calling to be the presence of Christ in our world, but it's going to take all congregations, nonprofits, and caring individuals to usher in real, sustainable transformation to our cities, towns, and neighborhoods. Affordable housing for all, food insecurity for no one, quality education and health care for everyone—even genuine spiritual renewal—are "do-able" IF we all do our part and follow the lead of God's Spirit.

Genuine gratitude for God's love and grace so freely given to us ought to be enough to launch us forward into this journey. It's not a magical "counting of our blessings" that transforms us into grateful people. It is a matter of humbling ourselves before the God of the universe and the One who holds all things together—all things seen and unseen. God alone is worthy of our praise. This God is the same God who created you "in his own image." Therefore, you have gifts, talents, skills, resources, and passions that God wants and expects you to use for God's glory and the benefit of others. So, with gratitude in your heart, use them—and push your

---

[27] Creasy Dean, *Innovating for Love.*

congregation to do the same.

Just know that whatever you try and whatever framework you choose to use will be flawed, and you will have plenty of mistakes awaiting you. But DO SOMETHING! Do what you can, with what you've been given, where you are.

If we pay attention to the winds of God's Spirit, then we will let go of the rudder, hoist our sails, and allow the Spirit to blow us to new places.

Every generation has its own stories to tell—whether it's walking five miles to school in the snow ... uphill ... both ways ... OR growing up without cable TV... or being deprived of owning your own cell phone until you were twelve years old. Yet, genuine gratitude usually works out like this: The more a person has experienced suffering or loss, disappointment or hurt, the more they choose to live with gratitude.

C.S. Lewis wrote: "God whispers to us in our pleasures, speaks in our conscience, but shouts in our pain: it is His megaphone to rouse a deaf world."[28]

And although we know this truth, it is a tremendous challenge to live every day as people who choose gratitude rather than feeling a shallow kind of "#Blessed!" As a Parkinson's patient, there are plenty of days when my body just will not do what I want it to do. It has been almost three years since I could just get up, grab a bag of golf clubs, and walk a few holes—something I did almost every evening for twenty years. But my body will not allow me to do it—and I live next to a golf course, which makes it even worse.

---

[28] C.S. Lewis, *The Problem of Pain* (HarperCollins, 2001).

There are days when I just want to scream and hide from the world. But I must get back up and do what I can with what I've been given, where I am at. I still have hopes of getting back on the golf course—no matter how ugly I play.

As I write these words, I am one year removed from three surgeries known as "Deep Brain Stimulation" (DBS), a process that offers hope for people living with Parkinson's disease. It is often referred to as a "pacemaker for the brain." DBS is not a cure, but it often relieves many of the worst symptoms for many people by interrupting targeted brain signals that are going to the wrong parts of the human body—at least that is my layman's understanding.

After three grueling surgeries, I am still waiting in hope for improvements to be fully realized. And honestly, it's driving me crazy! I am terrible at sitting around doing nothing. Yet here I am striving to be hopeful and grateful for this potential improvement in my quality of life—still to be determined. But that's enough about my story.

Now, I invite you to think about your story, and only you can write it. You are the author. I really hope you will take the time to be still and reflect on your life for a few moments, being guided by just five questions:

1. Where have you come from?
2. Where are you presently?
3. Where are you going?
4. In what ways does your story bring you gratitude?
5. How can you bless your community with your gifts?

Just write whatever comes to your mind. It cannot be wrong because it is your story. Geographically, spiritually, family, giftedness, passions, frustrations, disappointments, joys, aspirations, goals, and so on.

The same goes for your congregation. Gather a small group and try the same five questions from a congregational perspective. It could be an interesting discussion. Every congregation's story is different, but in God's creative wisdom and design, each strand of this diverse tapestry is woven together with love and gratitude to bring transformation to the communities in which we abide. Thanks be to God!

The following pages are purposefully left blank with questions at the top to prompt your thinking. The rest is up to you.

Where have you come from?

Where are you presently?

Where are you going?

In what ways does your story bring you gratitude?

How can you bless your community with your gifts?

Where has your congregation come from?

Where is your congregation presently?

Where is your congregation going?

In what ways does your congregation's story bring you gratitude?

How can your congregation bless your community with your gifts?

CHAPTER ELEVEN

Gratitude

It's Not Brain Surgery!

Comedian Jim Gaffigan does a hilarious take on "brain surgery"—not ordinarily a laughing matter—but he can do so because his wife had a brain tumor and is now well. She endured ten hours of successful brain surgery, and people assured him that this particular brain surgeon was the very best. Gaffigan quips:

> *"But isn't it enough that he's a brain surgeon? None of us could even get into med school. A brain surgeon goes to medical school, specializes in neurology, then in brain surgery, and we say, "Yeah, but are they any good?"*
>
> *"Yeah, they're a brain surgeon!"*
>
> *"Do you know what they do with the bad brain surgeons? They don't let them become brain surgeons."*
>
> *"Can you imagine the pressure they are under? At no point in their day can they say, Well, it ain't brain surgery! Because it's always brain surgery! Every day!"*

Experiencing gratitude inwardly and showing gratitude outwardly are not brain surgery. I have experienced both, and gratitude is much less invasive—at least physically. However, it does require a new heart and mind transformed by the spirit of God. We cannot produce gratitude in ourselves or in others. Gratitude is a gift from the God of abundance when one can see only scarcity. There is always more to the full picture that we cannot see, and that is why this journey into gratitude requires faith and trust.

My DBS surgery was not an instant fix. The brain is very complex, and my doctors tell me it could take twelve months or more before I know just how much, if any, of my Parkinson's symptoms might improve—then they remind you that not everyone who has DBS surgery has good results. Even if you do have positive results, it is not a cure. So far, my results have been disappointing.

Yet I am still hopeful that I can have a better quality of life. Even if it's not to my liking, I will adapt and continue onward in this journey with as much gratitude as I can muster. Some days, Parkinson's definitely kicks my butt—and more. Yet there are other days when gratitude wins. Basically, that is what it means to be human, even as we pursue the goal of gratitude in all circumstances. I hope to have more days when gratitude wins than when it doesn't.

So, let's take a quick review.

In this book, I have tried to be honest about my journey into gratitude with the heaviness of Parkinson's disease as my unwelcomed-but-constant companion.

In my view, we must take time to cultivate gratitude into our lives—not in a shallow prosperity-gospel kind of way, but rather, in the way of the One who was a suffering servant among us and revealed the way to live out the kingdom's values in his epic Sermon on the Mount.

Gratitude is not of our own creation, but we can choose to embrace it over despair and cynicism. It is God who creates a transformed heart and mind within us. We must do our part to cultivate an open, humble, and teachable spirit.

Ultimately, true gratitude is manifested in doing good to others out of gratitude for God's loving grace to us. And this is where the transformation happens—in us and through us as we make our way into the neediest parts of the communities in which we live. As we go with a spirit of gratitude to our brothers and sisters, that is precisely where we will find Jesus among us today.

Grat·i·tude: the quality of being ***thankful;*** readiness to show appreciation for and to return ***kindness.***

Here are a few final thoughts:

- Gratitude is more than a feeling, and it's not "all about me."
- If you choose gratitude as the lens through which you view life, it does NOT mean that:
    - o Your candidate will always win.
    - o That your life will be "#blessed."
    - o That your bank account will grow.
    - o That your life will be safe.
    - o That all your dreams will come true.
    - o That the best is yet to come.
    - o Or that you won't be diagnosed with Parkinson's—or worse.

Ephesians says very clearly:

> *Be kind and compassionate to one another, forgiving each other, just as in Christ God forgave you.*
>
> **Ephesians 4:32 (NIV)**

And Micah sums up God's expectations of us:

> *He has told you, O mortal, what is good; and what does the Lord require of you but to do justice, and to love kindness, and to walk humbly with your God?*
>
> **Micah 6:8 (NRSVue)**

But how can attributes like kindness, compassion, forgiveness, justice, and humility be lived out in the world today—especially when these godly traits are often mocked as weaknesses by those who lead us in government, society, and yes, unfortunately, in some congregations?

I would argue that these traits are a direct reflection of the upside-down kingdom of God. Jesus was painting an unmistakable picture of what a true disciple looks like in the Beatitudes:

> *When Jesus saw the crowds, he went up the mountain, and after he sat down, his disciples came to him. And he began to speak and taught them, saying:*
>
> *"Blessed are the poor in spirit, for theirs is the kingdom of heaven.*
>
> *"Blessed are those who mourn, for they will be comforted.*
>
> *"Blessed are the meek, for they will inherit the earth.*
>
> *"Blessed are those who hunger and thirst for righteousness, for they will be filled.*
>
> *"Blessed are the merciful, for they will receive mercy.*

"Blessed are the pure in heart, for they will see God.

"Blessed are the peacemakers, for they will be called children of God.

"Blessed are those who are persecuted for the sake of righteousness, for theirs is the kingdom of heaven.

"Blessed are you when people revile you and persecute you and utter all kinds of evil against you falsely on my account. Rejoice and be glad, for your reward is great in heaven, for in the same way they persecuted the prophets who were before you.

"You are the salt of the earth, but if salt has lost its taste, how can its saltiness be restored? It is no longer good for anything but is thrown out and trampled under foot.

"You are the light of the world. A city built on a hill cannot be hid. People do not light a lamp and put it under the bushel basket; rather, they put it on the lampstand, and it gives light to all in the house. In the same way, let your light shine before others, so that they may see your good works and give glory to your Father in heaven.

"Do not think that I have come to abolish the Law or the Prophets; I have come not to abolish but to fulfill. For truly I tell you, until heaven and earth pass away, not one letter, not one stroke of a letter, will pass from the law until all is accomplished. Therefore, whoever breaks one of the least of these commandments and teaches others to do the same will be called least in the kingdom of heaven, but whoever does them and teaches them will be called great in the kingdom of heaven.

For I tell you, unless your righteousness exceeds that of the scribes and Pharisees, you will never enter the kingdom of heaven."

Matthew 5:1-16 (NRSVue)

These characteristics must begin within us. And I would also suggest that when Jesus declared these poetic Beatitudes, he meant:

- They are not optional.
- They are not suggestions.
- Each one must be carried out with a spirit of humility.

Needless to say, Christians and churches in the United States have much intentional work to do! Maybe it begins with us declaring, "We will do the best we can with what we have been given, where we are at, and we will do this with a spirit of compassion, love, and gratitude." But where in the world do we begin?

The following quote is often attributed to Bishop Desmond Tutu of South Africa:

> *Every church should be able to get a letter of recommendation from the poor in their community.*

The quote seems to suggest that a congregation's very reputation hinges on its tangible care for the most vulnerable and marginalized in their community rather than on its worship style, number of young families with children it can claim, or size of the church's bank account. The quote suggests that a congregation's reputation in their community should be built on its tangible witness among the most vulnerable.

This does not mean the church should try to coerce the poor into providing a good reference. It also does not mean the church should not try to reach out to middle-class families or not strive to create the most meaningful worship services within its own capabilities and context.

Rather, it indicates a need for the church to change its focus. A church whose presence genuinely improves the lives of the poor won't need to ask for a letter of recommendation—the community's improved well-being will serve as a testament in itself.

I believe that authentic gratitude is born from love—love for God, love for people, and love for self in the healthiest kind of way. This is the way of transformation in us and in our communities. We can't fix Washington, D.C., but we can choose to bring gratitude, love, and basic human kindness instead of greed, hate, and divisiveness in our troubled world.

In his book, *Faith After Doubt,* Brian McLaren reminds us of a very important phrase expressed by Apostle Paul as he teaches revolutionary love to the Galatians:

> *For in Christ Jesus neither circumcision nor uncircumcision counts for anything; the only thing that counts is faith working through love.*
>
> **Gal. 5:6 (NRSVue)**

McLaren states:

> *According to many of our leading religious gatekeepers today Paul didn't get it quite right. He should have said, "For in Christ Jesus correct beliefs about circumcision and uncircumcision are still very important; the only thing that counts is faith expressing itself through correct beliefs." When he tries to summarize what God requires and desires, Paul does not say: "For the whole law is summed up in a single commandment, You shall have the correct beliefs." Rather, he declares, "For the whole law is summed up in a single commandment, 'You shall love your neighbor as yourself'"* (Galatians 5:14).
>
> *It appears that, for Paul, if you love your neighbor, the love*

> *of God is implied, assumed, included, or experienced as a byproduct, which, of course, echoes Jesus' words, that those who love "the least of these" actually love him.*[29]

So, how are we American Christians doing with that "love your neighbor" thing? Jesus never said, "You shall love the church," or "You shall love only those who agree with you."

He said, *Love God* AND *neighbor*—no exceptions. And he told his disciples to love in the same way that they had seen him love. Can't we see what is hidden in plain sight today? Not if we are looking through the lens of culture, politics, the economy, or power. We can only see what should be so obvious if we are looking through a lens of gratitude that is born of love. This is how transformation can happen in us and in our communities.

In my final sermon as a pastor of over thirty years, I tried to express my gratitude to the congregation, but words are not sufficient when it comes to remembering all the relationships forged through the living of life together—storms and all—as the Body of Christ.

As I fumbled through that sermon, I kept coming back to the word "gratitude" despite my liability and despite not wanting to end my ministry on these terms. I'm still on that journey, trying to live into this next season of life with gratitude each day. The truth is that I fall short more often than I succeed. But ultimately, I hope that you and I are choosing gratitude as our default setting for this journey of stumbling after the Jesus who laid out all we need to know in the Sermon on the Mount. Take the time to do a serious review of Matthew 5–7.

---

[29] Brian McLaren, *Faith After Doubt* (New York: St. Martin's Publishing, 2021).

Michael J. Fox, who has lived with Parkinson's disease for over thirty years, once said in an interview:

> *With gratitude, optimism is sustainable. If you can find something to be grateful for, then you will find something to look forward to. And you carry on.*[30]

I hear those words dripping with Christian hope! I encourage you to choose gratitude in the good times, in the difficult times, in the ordinary times, and in those times when you find yourself in that uncomfortable liminal space of transition.

In her final message, Julian of Norwich (1342-1430) was able to proclaim with humble boldness and gratitude: "And all will be well, all manner of things shall be well."[31] All shall be well. Maybe not to your liking, or mine, but God's universe will continue marching forward, and you will be held safely in the arms of a loving God.

As we continue to anxiously stand on the precipice of political elections, cultural and life transitions, and the uncertainties of the day, we would be wise to hear once again the words of Ephesians 4:32 and Micah 6:8:

> *Be kind and compassionate to one another, forgiving each other, just as in Christ God has forgiven you.*
>
> **Ephesians 4:32 (NIV)**
>
> *He has told you, O mortal, what is good; and what does*

---

[30] Jane Pauley, "Michael J. Fox on Parkinson's and How He Finds 'Optimism Is Sustainable,'" CBS News, April 30, 2023, accessed November 29, 2025, https://www.cbsnews.com/news/michael-j-fox-on-parkinsons-and-how-he-finds-optimism-is-sustainable/.

[31] Julian of Norwich, *Revelations of Divine Love, trans. Elizabeth Spearing* (London: Penguin Classics, 1998).

the Lord require of you but to do justice and to love kindness and to walk humbly with your God?

Micah 6:8 (NRSVue)

Try as we may, there is just no getting around kindness, justice, and humility for anyone who wishes to be called a child of God.

In Jesus' very first sermon, he chose the words of the prophet Isaiah that would guide his mission:

The Spirit of the Lord is upon me,
because he has anointed me
to bring good news to the poor.
He has sent me to proclaim release to the captives
and recovery of sight to the blind,
to let the oppressed go free,
to proclaim the year of the Lord's favor.

Luke 4:18-19 (NRSVue)

If this good news is to be experienced by the poor and the marginalized in our communities, by the oppressed and the captives of this world, and by those who cannot see, we had better find our way toward choosing a kind of gratitude, love, and compassion that leads us to new and fresh ways of being the presence of Christ in the same world that he lived and died for.

I thought about titling this book *Sh*t Happens—Try to Be Grateful!* But my better angels—and my publisher—prevailed (maybe that will be the sequel to this book). The point is that all too often we get too caught up in ourselves—too busy, too much pain, too much grief, too much politics, too much social media, and so on. The way out of that small-minded thinking is to be grateful and start doing something for others!

Just do what you can, with what you've been given, where you are, and it just might lead to your own transformation and the transformation of communities all across this land.

In this often-grueling journey of stumbling along after Jesus, it begins and ends best—and is lived most abundantly in between—when we begin choosing gratitude every day. May it be so in and through us.

With Gratitude,

Dennis Atwood

APPENDIX

Helpful Resources

- lakeinstitute.org/resource-library/story-shelf/gift-of-land-becomes-100k-for-community/
- cbf.net/sacredspaces
- data.census.gov/
- census.gov/acs/www/data/data-tables-and-tools/data-profiles/
- alban.org/uploadedFiles/Alban/Bookstore/pdf/resources/Asset_Mapping/resource2.pdf
- www.parkinson.org/
- www.michaeljfox.org/
- hope.cbf.net/who-we-are/
- www.sympara.org/
- welcomehouseraleigh.org
- resourceumc.org/en/content/agradecidos-en-toda-situacion
- livinglutheran.org/cultivating-a-grateful-heart/
- episcopalchurch.org/uto/strength-and-optimism-through-gratitude/

A SAMPLING OF GRATITUDE/THANKSGIVING

In Scripture

- Philippians 1:3
- 1 Thessalonians 3:9
- Colossians 3:15
- Hebrews 12:28
- 1 Corinthians 10:30
- Colossians 2:7; 3:15-16
- Philippians 4:6
- 1 Timothy 4:3
- 1 Chronicles 16:8
- Nehemiah 12:31
- Psalm 7:17; 28:7; 30:12; 35:18; 75:1; 95; 100; 107:1; 118:28; 136
- Romans 1:21
- 1 Corinthians 11:24; 15:57
- 2 Corinthians 2:14; 9:15
- 1 Thessalonians 5:18

www.ingramcontent.com/pod-product-compliance
Lightning Source LLC
LaVergne TN
LVHW010923110826
845149LV00013B/2456

* 9 7 9 8 9 9 4 2 0 0 8 0 3 *